NEW DIRECTIONS
FOR EXCEPTIONAL
CHILDREN

Number 5 • 1981

NEW DIRECTIONS FOR EXCEPTIONAL CHILDREN

A Quarterly Sourcebook
James J. Gallagher, Editor-in-Chief

Number 5, 1981

Socioemotional Development

Nicholas J. Anastasiow
Editor

Jossey-Bass Inc., Publishers
San Francisco • Washington • London

SOCIOEMOTIONAL DEVELOPMENT
New Directions for Exceptional Children
Number 5, 1981
Nicholas J. Anastasiow, Editor

New Directions for Exceptional Children is published
quarterly by Jossey-Bass Inc., Publishers. Subscriptions are
available at the regular rate for institutions, libraries, and
agencies of $30 for one year. Individuals may subscribe at the
special professional rate of $18 for one year.

Correspondence:
Subscriptions, single-issue orders, change of address notices,
undelivered copies, and other correspondence should be sent to
New Directions Subscriptions, Jossey-Bass Inc., Publishers,
433 California Street, San Francisco, California 94104.

Editorial correspondence should be sent to the Editor-in-Chief,
James J. Gallagher, Frank Porter Graham Child Development Center,
University of North Carolina, Chapel Hill,
North Carolina 27514.

Library of Congress Catalogue Card Number LC 80-84273
International Standard Serial Number ISSN 0271-0625
International Standard Book Number ISBN 87589-821-1

Cover design by Willi Baum
Manufactured in the United States of America

Contents

Socioemotional development involves the topics of emotions, temperament, affect, and attachment. This chapter examines these constructs and summarizes current research.

Socioemotional Development: The State of the Art

Nicholas J. Anastasiow

Imagine a reception at a national convention of the Council for Exceptional Children. The keynote speaker for the Division of Early Childhood Education has just addressed the membership. The keynote speaker's topic has been socioemotional development, and after the address several listeners drift into a discussion of the topic. At the beginning, the conversation is about how children gain the ability to relate to others. But at times the subject shifts to how children learn to control their emotions, adjust in school, delay gratification, sit still, pay attention, and not be aggressive.

Suddenly someone starts to talk about the reasons why modern children do not have better self-concepts. The speaker places the blame on parents. Another individual speaks about her recent experience in a Lamaze class and about the importance of establishing a strong bond between mother and child during the child's infancy. Another person, who has just finished a study, talks about emotions and their genetic base. This person states that emotions appear developmentally in all humans and serve as a way for infants to communicate, through individual temperamental differences, with their caregivers.

After this informal lecture, a teacher wants to discuss what he feels is really important for children—their ability to feel good about themselves and to express themselves creatively, with competence and trust in their own actions. He talks about Maslow's self-actualizing persons and confesses he has not met many. An overhearer insists that socioemotional development means having an adequate ego with mature coping mechanisms that allow the individual to do competent work and to love.

As the group disbands, a latecomer arrives. The latecomer is disappointed at having missed the keynote speech and asks for a summary of the salient points made about socioemotional development. The latecomer's request brings into sharp focus the fact that socioemotional development seems to mean a lot of different things to different people. The group realizes the diversity of opinions expressed: Socioemotional development means the development of emotions, the ability to get along with peers, the development of ego and superego, the ability to control emotions, the ability to work and love, the ability to form attachments and affiliations with caregivers and peers, and the ability to grow and develop as a person—in other words, it is a confusing puzzle.

Scientists who explore the field of socioemotional development and the wide assortment of topics that researchers have addressed may have the feeling of having peeled an onion layer by layer until there is no longer an onion. As Lewis and Rosenblum (1978) comment, "Research in child development over the last decade or two seems like a thousand lines of inquiry speading outward in an incoherent starburst of effort" (p. vii). This chapter addresses the basic incoherence of the starburst. One premise of this chapter is that as the lines of research have narrowed, the basic purpose behind this research has become blurred.

The stance of this chapter is that emotions, their expression, and their control by affect systems are the basic foundation of human behavior. When the course of development through infancy and childhood has been successful, the adult is capable of establishing loving relations and able to find satisfaction in work. This position is drawn from Freud (Vaillant, 1977). Freud's quality of success includes two facets—the ability to love and the ability to work. When Freud was only six months old, Tolstoy, in a letter to his fiancée, said it more eloquently: "One can live magnificently in this world, if one knows how to work and how to love, to work for the person one loves and to love one's work" (Vaillant, 1977, p. 8). These two abilities are at the heart of Western middle-class notions of success. The main issue in socioemotional development is how we gain the capacity to give and receive love and to work. The search for the elements that lead to this adult capability *is* the study of socioemotional development.

Major research is being conducted on social relations (see the chapter by Guralnick in this volume), self-concept (see the chapter by Anastasiow,

Grimmett, and Hanes), and the earlier sources of attachment and basic trust (see Ulrey's chapter). There is no clear, clean, good linkage among the topics. Lewis and Rosenblum's starburst is actually a set of shooting stars — researchers on different paths who occasionally gather at conferences to exchange their perceptions. The contention of this chapter is that socioemotional development is the foundation of the ultimate of all human capacities: the ability to love, which in turn is related to the ability to work.

It is not difficult to get lost in and lose sight of main threads in research that explores complex human behavior because almost everything comes into play — genes, environment, caregivers, social class. These global constructs mask core elements. In addition, it is not always easy to differentiate or identify what one finds at the core. The kernel of socioemotional development contains emotions, drives, and motives. As these three develop, they become intertwined with an affective control system that contains elements of cognition and a strong overlay of the values of the culture.

Although forewarned that the area is complex and untidy, the reader should remain aware that we are dealing with the most elegant of man's capacities. The difficulty of the search should not blind us to its immense potential benefits.

Mental Health

Mental health is the broad category under which most of the topics of socioemotional development can be grouped. The ways humans respond to stress or to the problems and demands of normal life can be seen as healthy or unhealthy. To be sure, one can argue definitions of the limits of mental health, but in general psychologists look at the manner in which humans respond to change and to stress. Vaillant (1977) quotes Frank Barron: "Mental health or soundness is a way of reacting to problems, not an absence of them" (p. 6). Vaillant studied 268 men from the Harvard class of 1942. Among those men who in their early fifties had established stable families and in the main achieved occupational distinction, there was not one who had enjoyed a life completely free of problems. Rather, the way in which these men had dealt with their problems defined their mental health. Although it may be an oversimplification, another way of stating the above is that research in socioemotional development seeks the sources of and the manner in which humans develop mental health.

Socioemotional development has been approached from several different perspectives. All but the followers of Skinner have tended to seek in infancy and childhood the principles or sources of the development of the individual's capacity to function effectively as an adult. The research in psychology for the past twenty years has been actively taking apart the human infant and the period of infancy. The notion held in the 1940s and the 1950s of a whole infant, globally perceived, masked the set of genetically based perceptual and cognitive competencies the child possessed at birth or developed during the first two decades of life.

Research in the field of infancy, as Lewis and Rosenblum (1978) point out, has produced a proliferation of information. Three selected reviews of the infant's general competency are those by Stone and others (1973), Osofsky (1979), and McCall (1979). More specific overviews on the talents of the infant include: hearing ability (Eisenberg, 1976); vision (Haith, 1979); sensorimotor development (Piaget's more than forty volumes, summarized by Piaget and Inhelder, 1969); motor development (Eichorn, 1979); social development (Sroufe, 1979); and emotional development (Emde and others, 1976). Some research laboratories have senior investigators, such as Michael Lewis at Educational Testing Service, examining the full range of cognitive, emotional, and social development during infancy. Currently, some investigators are trying to put our infant Humpty Dumpty together again as a whole child — a child who has genetic predispositions, who influences and is influenced by members of the environment, who has unique response rates, and who develops through alternate periods of relatively smooth learning and major reorganizations or shifts (Emde and others, 1976; Emde and Harmon, 1981).

The historical focus on infancy as a crucial time was an outgrowth of several factors. Of foremost influence is Freud's assertion that the developmental outcomes of infancy and early childhood are largely responsible for the quality of adult functioning. Freud felt that the base of achieving the capacity to love and to work rests in infancy and childhood and is in place by the child's fifth or sixth birthday. Freud's followers, in the main, have pursued infant/caregiver patterns of interaction and the development of the total person (the metaphor for the person's conception of the self being the ego). They have spent much energy examining the emotional components of their patients' talk regarding their early caregiver/child interactions (Rapaport, 1962). One of Freud's major contributions is the perspective that feelings, not facts, underlie adult neuroses and maturity. Feelings can become facts, but they may reside in the interpretations of events rather than in the events themselves.

Other researchers, such as Piaget, have pursued specific characteristics of cognitive development, and many measurement-oriented Americans have focused on IQ and its early predictors. In general, dynamic psychologists have pursued the emotional qualities related to the ability to love, while Piaget and other cognitive psychologists have pursued the intellectual components related to the ability to work. Dynamic psychologists are defined here as those psychologists interested in the internal psychic representations resulting from the transactions of biological states, genetic forces, and environmental events.

To dynamically oriented psychologists, such as Tomkins (1962), the emotions and the affect system developed through experience are the primary human system, and the drive system, important as it is, is secondary. Tomkins believes this position was very clear in Freud's early work but became reversed in his later writings when Freud suggested aggression as a drive. Thus, emotional development until recently has been the province of dynamically oriented psychologists, psychiatrists, and analysts (Ainsworth, 1979; Bowlby, 1969; Anna Freud, 1965; Rapaport, 1962; Spitz, 1959).

A related group of researchers are the social-learning theorists, with their interest in such constructs as dependency and guilt (Sears and others, 1957, 1965) and aggression and efficacy (Bandura, 1977). Again, underlying these research programs there is an implied interest in identifying those conditions in the childrearing patterns of infancy and childhood that lead to the type of adult functioning the culture deems successful (see particularly Vaillant, 1977).

Several longitudinal studies have followed infants into adulthood in an effort to explore those factors in childhood related to adult status. Principal among these have been the Berkeley Growth Study (Block, 1971), the Kauai Study (Werner and others, 1971; Werner and Smith, 1977, 1981), the Perinatal Collaborative Study in the United States (Broman and others, 1975), and the Newcastle upon Tyne Study (Neligan and others, 1974).

A more recent line of investigation has been to study the lives of people reared in stressful environments. There are studies of children from skid-row slums (Pavenstedt, 1967); children brought up in chronic poverty (Werner and Smith, 1981), including children of prisoners (Rutter, 1974); and children with schizophrenic mothers (Anthony and Koupernik, 1974). Out of this work has come the notion of competency or invulnerability in spite of known negative factors in the childrearing environment. These investigators have looked backwards to detect the factors that lead to adult neurosis and/or competence.

The analogy of the artist and the engineer may not be amiss here. Freud worked much as an artist works; he had global visions and made major inductive leaps from observations. Rarely did he work deductively. Out of Freud's theory, analysis developed, with its emphasis on the specifics in the growth and development of the child. Analysis probes the relationship of these specifics to the attainment of adult competency. That is, many of the investigations into the developmental process are attempts to discover and predict—and so "engineer"—the elements of human development. At the other extreme are those who reject Freudian theory, such as the behaviorists Watson (1924) and Skinner (1953). Both Watson and Skinner seek the principles of human development in the environment, yet they also work to engineer development. Less extreme but also empirically and behaviorally oriented are the social-learning theorists (Bandura, 1977; Sears and others, 1957, 1965) who also seek to identify principles of behavior in order to monitor development more competently.

Happily, except among an extreme group of behaviorists, there are a few points of agreement about development among psychologists. These general principles are:

- Development is a product of both genetic predispositions (maturation) and environmental responses to these dispositions (Emde and Harmon, 1981).
- Behavior is at any one time a product of genetics *and* environment; it is a product of all of one and all of the other. These elements cannot be separated (Freedman, 1979).
- Behavior is both emotionally and cognitively based. Cognition contains emotional overtones sometimes referred to as motivation, and affect contains a cognitive component (Yarrow, 1979).
- Development is bioadaptive. Its basic intent is survival. It is an evolving process rooted in the transactions between the infant and its primary caregiver—mother, father, grandparents, older siblings (Ainsworth, 1979; Bowlby, 1969).
- At a global or whole-person level, the product of development is autonomy—the ability to act independently, which is defined here as the ability to work—and competence—the capacity for self-acceptance and security or feelings of efficacy, which as defined here can be reduced to the ability to love friends, peers, lover, and self (Vaillant, 1977).
- Whereas human capacities are rooted in the evolutionary selective process transmitted by genes, the development of these capacities requires a social environment (Piaget and Inhelder, 1969).

This last generalization is a large one and has come to be accepted largely through the influence of Piaget and Inhelder (1969) and recent research (Emde and Harmon, 1981). It is composed of essentially two dynamically related parts—namely, that humans develop in social environments, and that the infant has the genetic capacity to be social. The research in this area focuses both on the infant's talents and on the talents of the caregiver in responding to the infant's needs. On the one hand, research seeks the course of development, and on the other hand, it looks at the caregiver's methods of facilitating development.

Many research studies could be selected as confirming evidence for this point, but let us examine Axelrad and Brody's (1978) longitudinal study. Axelrad and Brody examine the affective nature of what is developed in the child and how and when it is developed. They find that infants' general development "is a gradual accommodation to tension states, a gradual assimilation of new experiences, consistency and continuity of experiences, and a smoothly maintained balance of gratification and deprivation" (1978, p. 59). They believe parents need to shift with the changing demands of the infant-child, who moves from basic dependency in the first year of life through periods of independent assertions, new dependencies, and rebellious behavior in the first five years of life. In order to be accomplish new skills successfully, the child has an underlying need to be assured that he or she is loved.

Axelrad and Brody (1978) seek the environmental sources of the development of mature qualities in the seven-year-old and find that the major disruption to the child's ability to relate to and competently meet societal and internal demands is neglect in its various manifestations. That is, parental ignorance, disinterest, excessive indulgence, or carelessness do not facilitate the child's development.

Axelrad and Brody (1978), as well as many psychodynamically oriented researchers, look at the manner in which the child handles problems. These various manners are referred to as coping or defense mechanisms (Anna Freud, 1965; Murphy, 1962; Vaillant, 1977). Coping or defense mechanisms are postulated as innate human patterns for resolving conflict or satisfying needs. Thus, Axelrad and Brody seek the elements of developmental success in the early childhood period.

Axelrad and Brody's research covers a wide range of topics related to caregiver interaction and child characteristics, whereas other researchers in the socioemotional field have focused on individual topics. This chapter will examine three topics that are representative of current research efforts in the socioemotional field. These three are emotions, temperament, and attachment.

Emotions

Many articles on emotions begin by discussing such basic emotions as anger, fear, fury, anxiety, and shame and end by discussing how persons develop positive feelings about themselves (Yarrow, 1979). This approach illustrates how a basic human quality such as emotional capacity becomes intertwined with the attainment of a complex mature behavior such as an overall feeling of competence.

Izard's (1977) work identifies the basic emotions as pleasure, joy, anger, fear, guilt, and love. These emotions are agreed upon by most other researchers (Beckwith, 1979; Emde and others, 1976; Sroufe, 1979; Yarrow, 1979). Whereas some researchers are concerned with the expression of these emotions (Beckwith, 1979), others are attempting to identify their source and evolutionary function. These authors state that emotions are innate, appear in a regular sequence in all humans, and are genetically timed in their appearance analogously to fixed behavioral patterns (see also Emde and others, 1976).

Let us examine one emotional signal, the social smile, and note its appearance and possible function in evolutionary survival. The smile appears as early as seven months in premature infants. It also appears fleetingly in the first month of life of full-term infants and becomes more regular through the second month (Emde and others, 1976). Its occurrence is related to several physiological measures, such as brain wave patterns, rapid eye movements in sleeping and waking states, and heartbeat measures. These occurrences indicate the smile's relationship to environmental states. For most infants, the smile becomes stabilized at three months, when the infant consistently smiles at the face of the basic caregiver (Emde and others, 1976). Blind infants smile, although their smiles are somewhat less pronounced than smiles of sighted babies (Fraiberg, 1977; Freedman, 1979). The smile is genetically triggered and occurs probably without any conscious control by the infant.

It is only through transactions with the caregiver that the infant "learns" to smile and begins to appreciate situations in which to smile. Blind infants, because they do not receive the visual cues that "teach" them to smile, tend to stop smiling (Fraiberg, 1977; Freedman, 1979). Thus, the smile and the inferred state of contentment, pleasure, satisfaction, or the rarer expression of joy, serve to signal or communicate to the environment the infant's affective state. The smile engages the adult and stimulates the adult to talk to the infant and thus is also related to language development (Schaffer, 1977). Other behavioral indications of emotional state can be seen in universal facial expressions, for example, frowns, eye contact, or aversion (Campos, 1980).

There is further evidence of the innateness of emotions and the universality of the timing of their appearance. Sroufe (1979) has recently speculated on the timing of emotional development and notes that all emotions appear by the third year of life. Darwin was one of the first scientists to note, during his voyage on the *Beagle,* the similarities in the facial expressions that many different peoples use to show similar emotions. He raised the question of how people living without interpersonal contact learned to express the same emotions with the same facial expressions. Darwin speculated that emotions and their expressions must be genetic in origin.

Recent evidence demonstrates that infants in their first day of life display clear signs of a smile when a sweet-tasting substance is placed on their tongues, of a frown when a sour substance is introduced, and of refusal when a substance tasting, for instance, of rotten eggs is given (Steiner, 1979). These studies confirm both the inborn nature of taste sensation and the inborn communicative nature of the expressions. Steiner found further evidence that food and odor sensation is brain-stem (a part of the brain that evolved early) activity, as are the facial expressions accompanying them. Steiner (1979) has shown that severely retarded babies will display the same facial activities as normal neonates. Further, blind individuals, who have not seen facial expressions accompanying the presentation of food or an odor, will nonetheless display easily recognizable and appropriate facial expressions. (Steiner's work contains a set of pictures recommended to those interested in this topic.) The genetic origin of these expressions should not come as a surprise to those familiar with Marcel Marceau's or Charlie Chaplin's universally understood pantomimes.

Temperament

Individual differences in the expression of emotion are referred to as temperament (Goldsmith and Campos, 1981; Rothbart, 1973; Thomas and others, 1968). Temperament is an old construct found in the writings of Plato and Shakespeare; more currently, it appears in the body-type theories of attachment of Sheldon (1942) and in modern theories of attachment (Ainsworth, 1979). Goldsmith and Campos (1981) define temperament as a dispositional construct the refers to the *how* of behavior, not to the *what* or the *why*. Temperament can be measured behaviorally and has strong psychological correlates (Rothbart, 1973). Temperament is postulated to be the pattern of individual tendency to respond in a particular way (that is, irritably, passively, or pleasantly) and a commonly lifelong trait that deals with the intensity of response.

Temperament has become popularized recently in discussions of the Type A personality (intense, sullen, hard-working, serious) and the Type B personality (relaxed, easygoing, low-key) (Friedman and Rosenman, 1978). There appear to be social differences in temperament that can be measured in infants by their rates of response and irritability (Freedman, 1979). Chinese and Navajo infants at birth tend to be passive and far less irritable or excitable than Caucasians. These differences may have some implication for the dominant temperamental characteristics of Chinese and Navajo adults, who have been described as more passive and serene than Caucasians (Freedman, 1979). (For a full and current discussion on the topic of temperament, see Goldsmith and Campos, 1981; Rothbart, 1973; Thomas and others, 1968).

Emotions are the biological state and are accompanied by expressions of physiological correlates, such as increased heartbeat in excitation and fear (Campos, 1980). Affect is a more dynamic term. Affect includes the emotions and their physiological correlates, but the term *affect* includes the person's perception of the emotion and the person's cognitive interpretation of experience (Lewis and Rosenblum, 1978). Affect is a product of experience with emotions and a product of teaching and learning to interpret what the emotional states may mean. Thus, affective systems develop as self-systems develop, because a self is necessary to interpret emotions (Lewis and Rosenblum, 1978).

Humans are born with individual differences in response rates (temperament) and a set of basic emotions. Humans are also born with basic drives (food, air), which get expressed through emotions at certain temperament rates. Infant emotions are communications of drive needs and internal states. These emotions communicate to others what the infant needs. It is currently a popular view that the infant instigates the caregiver in the environment to resolve needs through the formation of attachment, to which we now turn.

Attachment

Attachment is the subject of at least three separate lines of research, that of the social-learning theorists of dependency (Sears and others, 1965), the ethologists (Lorenz, 1965), and the dynamic theorists, whose ideas grow out of notions of the negative effects of maternal deprivation and separation (Bowlby, 1969; Spitz, 1946). These last theorists postulate major decline in the infant's normal development if the child is separated from its basic caregiver sometime after five to six months of age and before the third birthday. From the deprivation-separation construct grew the notions of bonding and attachment (Bowlby, 1969; Spitz, 1946), and concepts from ethological studies were borrowed to explain human traits. For example, researchers studying birds found that early in the chick's life it would become attached to the dominant object in its perceptual field (Lorenz, 1965). Normally, goslings become attached to the goose who hatched the eggs, but they can also become attached to a surrogate mother chicken or to a human. The timing of attachment or bonding is very precise for most birds, and out of this fact has come the construct of the critical period and imprinting. Many researchers have investigated imprinting (bonding) and the notion of the critical period (see Sluckin, 1965, for an excellent summary).

Today, a more general point of view is held. It is now believed that attachment is a broader construct and should be considered as an attachment system (Emde and Harmon, 1981). Some theorists disagree that human attachment is more complex than animal attachment, but they are a minority among those who work on attachment (Cairns, 1972). The position taken by Bowlby (1969) and also heavily researched by Ainsworth (1979) is that the newborn infant is basically an affective behavioral system (Scarr-Salapatek, 1976). To survive, the infant needs warmth and security from the environment. The infant's genetic talents of cooing and smiling serve to evoke caregiving from the attending adults. By caring for the infant, the caregiver sets up a system of interaction that tends to build attachment between the infant and the caregiver and, gradually, between the child and other adults. The basic caregiver is usually a woman, most frequently the biological mother, but it can also be a surrogate mother or the father. Theorists postulate that out of the caretaking affiliation system, the infant builds a sense of autonomy and competence.

Exceptionality and Socioemotional Development

This volume explores socioemotional development in its special application to the exceptional person. Ulrey discusses the process of the establishment of individuation (another construct for self) and how the child's exceptionality may interfere with the smooth flow of that process. Anastasiow, Grimmett, and Hanes (this volume) discuss the development of self-concept and the influence of environment on that development. The chapter by Guralnick discusses attempts to normalize social experiences for exceptional children. Ziarnik's chapter discusses a training technique that helps handicapped adolescents acquire strategies for successfully negotiating the demands of the social environments so that they can work in normalized settings. Ziarnik's techniques help the adolescent achieve acceptance by others and, by extension, self-acceptance.

Those in the field of exceptionality attempt to improve the lives and life chances of those who have sensory, perceptual, motor, or cognitive deficits. These people are called handicapped; they are in great part handicapped by the constraints imposed on them by the environment. The chapters that follow suggest that it is possible not only to improve the skills of impaired persons to enable them to master the environment but also to enhance their self-respect and self-acceptance so that they may acquire the ultimate human capacity, the capacity to love.

References

Ainsworth, M. S. "Infant-Mother Attachment." *American Psychologist,* 1979, *34* (10), 932–937.

Anthony, E. J., and Koupernik, C. (Eds.). *The Child in His Family: Children at Psychiatric Risk.* Vol. 3. New York: Wiley, 1974.

Axelrad, S., and Brody, S. *Mothers, Fathers, and Children.* New York: International Universities Press, 1978.

Bandura, A. *Social Learning Theory.* Englewood Cliffs, N.J.: Prentice-Hall, 1977.

Beckwith, L. "Prediction of Emotional and Social Behavior." In J. Osofsky (Ed.), *Handbook of Human Development.* New York: Wiley, 1979.

Block, J. *Lives Through Time.* San Rafael, Calif.: Bancroft Books, 1971.

Bowlby, J. *Attachment and Loss.* Vol. 1. *Attachment.* New York: Basic Books, 1969.

Broman, S., Nichols, P. L., and Kennedy, W. A. *Preschool IQ.* Hillsdale, N.J.: Erlbaum, 1975.

Cairns, R. "Attachment and Dependency." In J. Gewirtz (Ed.), *Attachment and Dependence.* New York: Holt, Rinehart and Winston, 1972.

Campos, J. J. "Emotional Development." Developmental Psychobiology Group Lecture, University of Colorado Medical School, Denver, 1980.

Eichorn, D. "Physical Development: Current Foci on Research." In J. D. Osofsky (Ed.), *Handbook of Infant Development.* New York: Wiley, 1979.

Eisenberg, R. B. *Auditory Competence in Early Life: The Roots of Communicative Behavior.* Baltimore, Md.: University Park Press, 1976.

Emde, R. N., Gaensbauer, T. J., and Harmon, R. J. *Emotional Expression in Infancy: A Biobehavioral Study.* New York: International Universities Press, 1976.

Emde, R. N., and Harmon, R. J. *Attachment and Affiliative Systems: Neurobiological and Psychobiological Aspects.* New York: Plenum, 1981.

Fraiberg, S. *Insights from the Blind.* New York: Basic Books, 1977.

Freedman, D. G. *Human Sociobiology.* New York: Free Press, 1979.

Freud, A. *Normality and Pathology in Childhood.* New York: International Universities Press, 1965.

Friedman, M., and Rosenman, R. H. *Type A Behavior and Your Heart.* New York: Fawcett, 1978.

Goldsmith, H. H., and Campos, J. J. "Toward a Theory of Infant Temperament." In R. N. Emde and R. J. Harmon (Eds.), *Attachment and Affiliative Systems: Neurobiological and Psychobiological Aspects.* New York: Plenum, 1981.

Haith, M. M. "Visual Cognition in Early Infancy." In R. B. Kearsley and I. E. Sigel (Eds.), *Infants at Risk: Assessment of Cognitive Functioning.* Hillsdale, N.J.: Erlbaum, 1979.

Izard, C. E. (Ed.). *Human Emotions.* New York: Plenum, 1977.

Lewis, M., and Rosenblum, L. A. (Eds.). *The Development of Affect.* Vol. 1. *Genesis of Behavior.* New York: Plenum, 1978.

Lorenz, K. L. *Evolution and Modification of Behavior.* Chicago: University of Chicago Press, 1965.

12

McCall, R. *Infants.* Cambridge, Mass.: Harvard University Press, 1979.

Murphy, L. B. *The Widening World of Childhood: Paths Toward Mastery.* New York: Basic Books, 1962.

Neligan, G., Prudham, D., and Steiner, H. *Formative Years: Birth, Family, and Development in Newcastle upon Tyne.* Oxford, England: Oxford University Press, 1974.

Osofsky, J. D. (Ed.). *Handbook of Infant Development.* New York: Wiley, 1979.

Pavenstedt, E. *Children of Disorganized Lower-Class Families: The Drifters.* Boston: Little, Brown, 1967.

Piaget, J., and Inhelder, B. *The Psychology of the Child.* New York: Basic Books, 1969.

Rapaport, D. *The Structure of Psychoanalytic Theory.* Psychological Issues Monograph 6. New York: International Universities Press, 1962.

Rothbart, M. "Laughter in Young Children." *Psychological Bulletin,* 1973, *80,* 247–256.

Rutter, M. "Epidemiological Strategies and Psychiatric Concepts in Research on the Vulnerable Child." In E. J. Anthony and C. Koupernik (Eds.), *The Child in His Family: Children at Psychiatric Risk.* Vol. 3. New York: Wiley, 1974.

Scarr-Salapatek, S. "An Evolutionary Perspective on Infant Intelligence: Species Patterns and Individual Variations." In M. Lewis (Ed.), *Origins of Intelligence.* New York: Plenum, 1976.

Schaffer, H. R. *Studies in Mother-Infant Reaction.* New York: Academic Press, 1977.

Sears, R. R., Maccoby, E., and Levin, H. *Patterns of Childrearing.* New York: Harper & Row, 1957.

Sears, R. R., Rau, L., and Alpert, R. *Identification and Childrearing.* Stanford, Calif.: Stanford University Press, 1965.

Sheldon, W. H. *The Varieties of Temperament.* New York: Harper & Row, 1942.

Skinner, B. F. *Science and Human Behavior.* New York: Free Press, 1953.

Sluckin, W. *Imprinting and Early Experience.* Hawthorne, N.Y.: Aldine, 1965.

Spitz, R. A. "Anaclitic Depression." *Psychoanalytic Study of Children,* 1946, *2,* 313–342.

Spitz, R. A. *A Genetic Field Theory of Ego Formation: Its Implications for Pathology.* New York: International Universities Press, 1959.

Sroufe, L. A. "The Coherence of Individual Development: Early Care, Attachment, and Subsequent Developmental Issues." *American Psychologist,* 1979, *34* (10), 834–841.

Steiner, J. E. "Human Facial Expressions in Response to Taste and Smell Stimulation." *Advances in Child Development and Behavior,* 1979, *13,* 257–295.

Stone, J., Smith, H., and Murphy, L. *The Competent Infant.* New York: Basic Books, 1973.

Thomas, A., Chess, S., and Birch, H. G. *Temperament and Behavior Disorders in Children.* New York: New York University Press, 1968.

Tomkins, S. S. *Affect-Imagery-Consciousness.* Vols. 1 and 2. New York: Springer, 1962.

Vaillant, G. E. *Adaptation to Life.* Boston: Little, Brown, 1977.

Watson, J. B. *Psychology: From the Standpoint of a Behaviorist.* Philadelphia: Lippincott, 1924.

Werner, E. E., Bierman, J. M., and French, F. E. *The Children of Kauai.* Honolulu: University Press of Hawaii, 1971.

Werner, E. E., and Smith, R. S. *Kauai's Children Come of Age.* Honolulu: University Press of Hawaii, 1977.

Werner, E. E., and Smith, R. S. *Vulnerable, but Invincible: A Longitudinal Study of Resilient Children and Youth.* New York: McGraw-Hill, 1981.

Yarrow, L. J. "Emotional Development." *American Psychologist,* 1979, *34* (10), 951–947.

Nicholas J. Anastasiow is professor of psychiatry and associate director for research at the John F. Kennedy Child Development Center, University of Colorado Health Sciences Center. He was formerly director of the Institute for Child Study at Indiana University.

Value differences in self-concept may be confused with exceptionality. This chapter reviews how self-concept is developed and in turn in influenced by social class and minority group values.

Ethno- and Social-Cultural Differences in Self-Concept Development

Nicholas J. Anastasiow
Sadie Grimmett
Michael L. Hanes

Self-concept and self-esteem, as psychological constructs, have been central mechanisms proposed for understanding human functions (Maslow, 1962; Poppard and Eccles, 1977; Rodgers and Dymond, 1954). These constructs have also played a dominant role in the attempt to understand children and their success or lack of success in school (Sears, 1963; Shavelson and others, 1976; Wylie, 1975). From an educational point of view, each construct may be important in understanding variations of children's academic achievement (Shavelson and others, 1976). However, a number of theoretical and methodological issues remain unsolved by the research studies examining the development of children's perceptions of themselves (Wylie, 1975). Further, at the theoretical level, researchers have used different basic definitions for self-concept and self-esteem; therefore, conclusions across studies are difficult to integrate because of differing assumptions.

A related unsolved problem is understanding the development of children's self-concepts and identifying the significant variables that influence children's self-perceptions. Although a stage sequence of a child's development of self-perception has been proposed by Elkind (1978), little is known about the stages, if they indeed exist.

The most frequently discussed concerns in research are the measurement and interpretation of the scores obtained on self-esteem and self-concept instruments and whether they are valid measures of the child's self-perceptions. For instance, one might question the validity of some instruments that measure self-concept because of the assumption that the total score on the instrument reflects the same construct for all children who respond to the individual items on that instrument. This may be a faulty assumption because attitudes toward self appear to be developed within the social context in which the child is reared. Thus, items on measures of self-concept will take on different values depending upon the race, ethnicity, and sex of the child.

We believe self-concept develops much as the anthropologists believe social growth occurs; that is, through the two mechanisms of cultural affiliation and membership (Freedman, 1979). Both cultural affiliation and membership are achieved through the process of enculturation. Enculturation is a process of adapting to one's culture. In the context of childhood, it is commonly called socialization.

If we could strip away the culture, we would expect to find processes by which the individual organizes drives, motives, and emotions into some type of self or ego. Of course, such stripping away is impossible. Yet in essence we use the stripping-away process when we assume that the effects of different ethnocultures and sociocultures are the same and that all children come to school with commonly shared values.

This chapter focuses on the differences in the way children from different ethnocultures respond to statements about themselves. The chapter also explores relationships among their responses. Self-concept reflects personal values. Values developed in a social context will vary from social class to social class and among ethnic groups. Therefore, major differences in the way the notion of self is constructed should exist among children in different ethnocultures and sociocultures. We believe it is necessary to sort out these basic differences among ethnic and social groups' manner of structuring self-concept before we can examine the impact of exceptionality on the construction. At the end of the chapter we will discuss these issues as they relate to the exceptional child.

Self-Concept: Some Definitions

In education and psychology, the construct of self has been referred to as ego (Freud's *des Ich*), self-concept, and self-esteem (Kelly, 1955; Loevinger, 1976; Maslow, 1962; Sears, 1963; Sullivan, 1953). Loevinger (1976) gives an excellent review of these multiple and somewhat overlapping definitions and removes ego to a different sphere from self-concept. The ego, in Loevinger's view, "is a *process, structure, social* in origin functioning as a *whole* and guided by *purpose* and *meaning*" [emphasis added] (p. 67). Self-concept is subordinate to, and a more limited construct than, ego.

For Shavelson and others (1976), the self-concept is a person's self-perception, which is organized, multifaceted, hierarchical, stable, developmental, evaluative, and differentiable. Shavelson and others suggest that the category system adopted by an individual is to some degree a reflection of the individual's culture. Further, these organized experiences reflect the opinions or attitudes of a particular facet of an individual or cultural subgroup. Shavelson and others propose that self-concept is situation specific and generally stable over time, becomes more complex with experience and maturation, can be identified as an aspect of personality, and contains an evaluative component. Note that this account does not describe the self-concept as a process, an attribute that Loevinger (1976) attributes to the ego. Thus, *ego,* in Loevinger's sense, is close to the notion of self-concept proposed by Shavelson and others, but the two are not isomorphic.

In philosophy and neurology, notions of the self are usually embedded in the mind-body issue, with current opinion clearly on the side of a separate self that is a product of development and eventually becomes "the pilot of the ship (the body)" (Poppard and Eccles, 1977, p. 105). The separation of self and body is reflected in the title of Poppard and Eccles' work, *The Self and Its Brain.* Less concern is given to the actual definitions of self by Poppard and Eccles, who propose the existence of a self in charge of a machine (the body). Their position on how the self develops, however, is very close to the position expounded in cognitive constructionist theory.

As we will discuss in the following sections, self-perceptions are not exact representations of either past or present experiences. The significant point is that self-perceptions are a product of the individual's cognitive functioning, which is influenced by social and physical transactions with the environment and by maturation. While the distinction between self-concept and self-esteem may be useful for empirical purposes, the following discussion emphasizes that the development of self-perceptions, both self-concept and self-esteem, are equally influenced by the same factors.

In this chapter, the construct of self will be limited to the definition provided by Shavelson and others (1976): "Self-concept is a person's perception of himself" (p. 411). Perception, in this case, includes content information (for instance, "I am a football player") and feelings about the content (for instance, "I am a good football player"). A significant point, however, is that self-perceptions are not necessarily accurate interpretations of either past or present experiences in the environment because self-perceptions are seen as the product of an individual's cognitive functioning.

Development of Self-Perceptions

Poppard and Eccles (1977) perceive the earliest development of the self in the infant's genetic push to regard faces. From these earliest perceptions, they suggest, the infant comes to know the mother's face and, hence, later his or her own. Psychologists describe this process as differentiation of the self from the mother (Spitz, 1946). Current opinion among psychologists is that the emergence of the self as differentiated from the mother occurs around the age of eight months (Piaget and Inhelder, 1969; Schaffer, 1977; see also Ulrey's chapter in this book).

Whether differentiation of the self from the mother is the result of a genetic tendency or whether it is one aspect of general cognitive functioning, a logical assumption is that knowledge about the self is constructed by the child from his or her interactions with the environment. Derived from cognitive theory, this position maintains that each individual constructs a personal reality based on the utilization of schemata or cognitive structures (Bartlett, 1958; Gibson, 1969; Neisser, 1967; Piaget, 1970). According to Piaget, the schemata present at birth are in the form of sensory motor reflexes that provide a basis for interacting with the environment. Additional schemata are developed and become modified as a function of two factors: experience with the environment and genetically controlled maturation of sensory systems. Thus, as an individual has more experiences over time, initial schemata are modified into more complex structures that function in perception, attention, and other cognitive processes related to thinking (Anderson and others, 1977; Neisser, 1967).

In this view, schemata are an internalized reality constructed by the individual. Poppard and Eccles (1977) refer to this as "a second world." The internalized reality, however, is not a duplicate of the actual environment but an idiosyncratically constructed view (Jerison, 1976). The internalized view constructed by each individual is shaped by the activities of that individual within an environment and the interpretation of the events provided by the social agents in the environment. The manner in which agents provide interpretation is the generally accepted "socialization process" by which each member of a group comes to interpret reality in terms of the common values, attributes, and beliefs held by the group (Kerckhoff, 1972; Mead, 1934). This social-environmental feedback is viewed as a significant influence in the development of the self. That is, the self "is seen," as Sullivan (1953) describes it, through the reflected appraisal of the significant others in the environment.

An additional factor in the development of self is the qualitative changes that result from cognitive restructuring. The effect of the restructuring process on the content and characteristics associated with self-perceptions have been noted in developmental studies. As one result of cognitive development, the child develops a capacity for self-awareness and self-reflection (Poppard and Eccles, 1977). Even the young child is aware of the individual differences in physical build and appearance. It would appear that the notions or self-perceptions that individuals develop about themselves are the clearest examples of self-concepts.

Children are not only conscious of and develop complete notions about the self, but they also develop associated self-perceptions or feelings about their goodness, badness, rightness, or wrongness. In the language of current research, the affective feelings that an individual develops about the self constitute an individual's self-esteem (Sears, 1963). As Sears indicates, self-esteem may be positive or negative, but as a construct, self-esteem refers to the judgment persons have of themselves.

The previous discussion has focused on three factors that are related to the development of self-perceptions: (1) environmental interactions, (2) appraisals by significant others, and (3) developmental changes in cognitive processing (Mead, 1934; Sullivan, 1953; Wylie, 1975). The following section examines these factors as they are operationally defined in the research literature.

Research on Self-Perceptions

Much of the research literature focuses on demonstrating differences in self-perceptions between groups of children. In these studies, children with negative self-concepts have been characterized as passive rather than active, externally controlled as opposed to internally controlled, and more anxious than children with positive self-concepts (Cohen, 1976; Coopersmith, 1967). Since these differential characteristics are used to account for achievement differences among children and social class groups (Marx and Winne, 1975; Wylie, 1975), self-concept is expected to covary with these factors. The results from studies of self-concept and academic achievement, however, are mixed (Wylie, 1975). Some studies report a positive relationship (Coopersmith, 1967; Purkey, 1970), while others report no relationship (Marx and Winne, 1975). Similarly, there appears to be conflicting evidence relating self-concept differences and different social class groups (Kerckhoff, 1972; Soares and Soares, 1969; Trowbridge, 1972).

There is some evidence to suggest that a child's self-perception is affected by situational or contextual variables. As an example, Caplin (1969), in a study of fourth-, fifth-, and sixth-grade children, reports that the school setting influenced only school-related self-concept, while personal self-concept was not influenced. A review of the literature on the impact of school desegregation on self-concept indicates mixed findings. Roughly half the studies report a positive relationship; the remaining studies report no relationship or a negative relationship (Weinberg, 1977). The importance of situational variables is reinforced, however, by the evidence that the child's perception of the relation-ship between the school environment and self-concept can be identified as classroom specific (Rogers and others, 1978; Sears and Sherman, 1964).

Self-concept differences among racial-ethnic groups have long been presumed. The most frequent comparisons have been between blacks and anglos; some investigators document differences (Attemborough and Zdep, 1973; Powers and others, 1971; Soares and Soares, 1969), but others find no differences (Carter, 1968; Healey and DeBallasie, 1974). Weinberg (1977), who reviewed black and anglo comparative studies of self-concept for many different age groups, found that half of thirty-four studies of self-concept showed black self-concept was as high as or higher than white self-concept; in seven cases, self-concept was equal between the races; and in ten, black self-concept was as low as or lower than that of whites.

Although a number of methodological problems may account for the inconsistency in research findings, the prevailing problem may be the basic conception of self-concept and self-esteem as unitary and relatively stable con-structs. There is support for a more complex view of self-concept and self-esteem — for instance, Monge's (1973) study of self-concept structure stability as a function of age and sex differences and Wober's (1971) work on the differ-ences in self-evaluative criteria accepted by different cultural groups.

Epstein (1974) notes that an individual's self-esteem is a subsystem of internally consistent, hierarchically organized concepts. Epstein also says that self-esteem is a dynamic organization that changes with experience. Thus to the extent that two or more individuals' experiences have been similar (or dif-ferent), their self-concepts might be expected to show similar (or different) pat-terns, both in terms of relative position and relative power. Positive or nega-tive reactions to a statement such as "My teacher thinks that I am a good stu-dent" are thus not very meaningful without knowledge of their relationship to the overall system. The most cogent question concerning self-esteem and eth-nic group membership then becomes one of discerning the pattern differences and identifying or establishing their validity in terms of the referent system for each ethnic group.

In terms of the origin, development, and cognitive structuring of self-concept and self-esteem, there is some evidence to suggest that pattern differ-ences are influenced by the feedback from significant people and by experi-ences within the environment. That is, the organization of self-concept and self-esteem reflects the experiences of the child within a particular social group as well as the attitudes and values of that social group.

The following sections examine social influences on the structure of children's self-perceptions. Of particular interest in these sections is the means by which social variables are influential and the specific content that social agents communicate to the child.

Cultural Context of Self

A pervasive social influence on the developing self-perception is culture. Two prominent cultures for the family are its social class (Kerckhoff, 1972) and ethnic group (Kiefer, 1974; Matthews, 1965; Ramirez and Castaneda, 1974; Weinberg, 1977). Social class and ethnic group each connote shared ways of thinking, believing, and feeling—ways that are stereotypic for persons who are members of that group. This definition of social class and ethnic group are synonymous with culture (Goldschmidt, 1967; Kluckhohn, 1962). To avoid this confusion we will identify social class as socioculture and ethnicity as ethnoculture.

Functionally, culture is the macrosetting for inputting and discerning balance, value, efficacy of social actions. Cultural continuity is achieved when children are socialized according to the implicit premises of the culture. That is, socialization maximizes the compatibility of their behavioral patterns, beliefs, and values with cultural meanings (Hall, 1976; Hershovitz, 1973). As one result, the child's developing self-perception is influenced by each family member who acts as a mediator between the child and the referent culture. As a mediator, the family communicates at least two cultures, an ethnoculture and a socioculture, from which the child constructs a conception of self.

In a society, ethnoculture and socioculture intersect such that the values, beliefs, and behavioral patterns of each commingle. Ethnocultures sharing the same socioculture would therefore have some common beliefs, while other beliefs would be distinctive to the ethnoculture. An ethnoculture composed of different sociocultures will have common and distinctive beliefs; the different beliefs are the result of the influence of each socioculture. For instance, the notion of work is shared across middle and lower classes. However, the outcomes of work are perceived quite differently by the two classes.

In the process of communicating culture, the family's unique traditions, patterns, and values provide or imply the definitions of family membership and the individual's role in the family. In essence, each child develops from those unique patterns of his or her family (Schachtel, 1959). Looff (1971) reports that family tradition is an important component in interpreting a family member's behavior for anglos residing in Appalachia. Unique familial patterns, such as those discussed by Looff, have been suggested as the source of achievement differences in children from the same social class (Shipman, 1977). In a longitudinal study of Head Start children, Shipman found that some families had a tradition of hard work and that this striving was related to the child's achievement in school. In addition, Berkowitz (1964) argues that family culture is the source of self-concept differences for nondelinquent children residing in a community with a high delinquency rate. Thus, the evidence supports the position that the family makes unique and significant contributions to the child's development of self-perceptions. There are, then, three simultaneous cultural influences on the self-concept: ethnoculture, socioculture, and family.

It is assumed that the child constructs a view of self from transactions initially with significant family members and later with significant persons in other social contexts. We assume that during the first five years of life or before the child attends school, the family has the greatest impact on the development of the child's self-concept. Following this period, the child's environment in school and others, adults and peers, who represent the culture have significant influence on the child's self-concept. This second influence causes changes in the self-concept away from a more idiosyncratic family representation of the ethnoculture toward a broader perspective of the culture at large. A child's transactions and their relationship to the development of self-perceptions are products both of the transactions the child engages in and the child's self-perceptions.

That is, a transaction can be influenced by self-produced determinants as well as situational determinants (Bandura, 1978; Endler and Magnusson, 1976). In addition, children engaged in the same transaction or similar transactions select the particular aspect of the transaction that is important to the self. For example, two children given a workbook assignment might react differently. The first child's self-concept might make being first to complete the assignment important, whereas the other's self-concept might make being accurate important. These two children are constructing their views of self uniquely, although the transaction is a shared one.

The nature of the transaction will depend upon such personal characteristics as sex and age. Girls and boys experience different social contexts (Baumrind, 1972; Hoffman, 1961; Kerckhoff, 1972) as well as different physioanatomical information. Clearly, these differences may affect the development of self-perceptions (Sears, 1963). Also, as children grow older, they experience social interactions outside of the family (Kerckhoff, 1972) and acquire greater cognitive maturity (Piaget and Inhelder, 1969; Werner, 1957). The expanded social environment increases the diversity of information about the self and about what is valued in one's own culture and other cultures. Greater cognitive maturity enhances the child's control when he or she constructs experiences and selects those situations that are important to him or her. With reference to the selection of experience, Bandura (1978) concludes that "it is mainly in areas affecting one's welfare and self-esteem that favorable performance appraisals activate personal consequences" (p. 349). Because with age the child increasingly controls the experiences that affect his or her welfare, greater cognitive complexity may provide for an increasingly stable as well as differentiated self-perception.

Theoretically, this gradual differentiation will reflect familial, ethnocultural, sociocultural, and personal beliefs and values about the self that are identifiable in the child's self-report. One would expect common patterns of beliefs about the self in children belonging to the same ethnoculture; one would also expect those patterns to provide evidence of the beliefs and values held by that ethnoculture. Common self-perception patterns across ethnocultures and within social status levels reflect shared sociocultural beliefs and values about the self, which are discussed in the next section.

Sociocultural Values

Value differences among social classes or sociocultures are well accepted; a common contrast is the one made between middle-status and lower-status sociocultures (Kerckhoff, 1972). The value themes of these two sociocultures that seem most relevant to self-perception will be discussed in the next section. We were guided by common sense and intuition in selecting the values for analysis. As Tyler (1978) says, "There is no universal catalogue of human values and no established criteria for pruning . . . to make sure nothing essential is being omitted" (p. 132). Moreover, the selected themes are conceptualized as components of a value structure (Rokeach, 1973) in which differential weighting is given to various values. As a consequence, specific comparisons of themes should be considered relative to the value structure (Tyler, 1978).

Our discussion of sociocultural values draws on Papajohn and Spiegel's (1975) model of value structure. Their model includes five value sets, four of which are listed in Table 1. The fifth value set in Table 1, *Assistance,* was developed by the authors. The *Activity* value set refers to the group's concern for the manner in which the individual expresses the self in the world. *Relationships* refers to the manner in which individuals within groups relate to each other through roles or kinships. The *Time* value set refers to the group's time orientation: past, present, or future. *Man-Nature* refers to the value set regarding man's mastery or coexistence with nature. A fifth set, *Assistance,* has been developed to expand the value model to include prosocial behavior. The *Assistance* value set refers to values about helpfulness and the concern for another person's welfare. This set has been added in view of the growing recognition of prosocial behavior as a basic activity of man (Fishbein, 1976) and the increasing attention psychologists are giving this domain (Rosenhan, 1972; Staub, 1978).

Presented in Table 2 are the differences in value orientation of the middle- and lower-status sociocultures. The middle class values *Individuality* relative to *Collaterality* and *Lineality; Doing,* the *Future,* and *Mastery* are prized more than other themes in the respective sets (Kerckhoff, 1972; Papajohn and Spiegel, 1975). The concern for individuality in the middle class is reflected in a belief in private property including, according to Bernstein (1972), information. Belief in independence (Baumrind, 1972; Hoffman, 1972), self-assertive-

Table 1. Value Set and Themes

Value	Themes		
Activity*	*Doing* Action measured by standards of achievement	*Being* Action expresses personality	*Being-in-becoming* Action develops the whole self
Relationship*	*Individuality* Reciprocal roles based on individual independence	*Collaterality* Reciprocal roles based on group interdependence; egalitarian, horizontal relations	*Lineality* Reciprocal roles based on superordinate-subordinate, vertical, authoritarian relations
Time*	*Future* Emphasis on to be; planning and deciding what is yet to come	*Present* Emphasis on now; plan for immediate goal	*Past* Emphasis on tradition; plan for continuation of what has been
Man-Nature*	*Mastery* Effort can overcome nature	*Subjugation* Effort cannot counteract nature	*In harmony* Effort agrees with nature; is coextensive
Assistance	*Competency* Helpfulness indicates personal skill	*Compassion* Helpfulness indicates concern for another's welfare	*Obligation* Helpfulness due to being "good," moral

*Adapted from Papajohn and Spiegel (1975).

ness, initiative, and self-control (Kerckhoff, 1972) exemplifies the importance of individuality in the middle class.

Related to valuing individuality is the emphasis on *Doing* by the middle class, rather than the lower-class emphasis on being. Actions directed toward overcoming obstacles and resolution of problems are valued more than actions primarily expressing one's personality. This focus on doing is revealed in early socialization practices stressing achievement motivation, which are prominent in the middle class (Hoffman, 1972; McClelland and others, 1953). Doing also implies concomitant values about the task and its importance and difficulty; about the task outcome, that is, success or failure; and about the time frame for accomplishment.

The time frame of the middle class is futuristic. The child is educated with a view toward the future (Bernstein, 1972). In addition, there seems to be continued anticipation that future lifeways will be bigger and better (Papajohn and Spiegel, 1975).

In contrast, the lower-class values present time more than future time as implied by the concern for being, as expressed in family comfort more than for family security (Rokeach, 1973). Doing is valued but is anchored to authoritarian relations; this authoritarian orientation is perhaps the result of the functional realism of subjugated economic and occupational roles (Kerckhoff, 1972).

Interpersonal sensitivity or an expression of personal concern and interest in others is important to the lower-status sociocultural groups (Looff, 1971; Ramirez and Castaneda, 1974). Middle-class persons are likely to place less emphasis on assistance values, which they may perceive to conflict with the valuing of individuality (Staub, 1978). Lower-class persons, however, express much warmth and consideration in their interpersonal relations, particularly with trusted persons. The family encourages manifestation of feelings among its members, and such demonstrations of affect are a major vehicle for exhibiting one's personality (Looff, 1971).

The lower-class emphasis on politeness and obedience (Rokeach, 1973) reflects the importance of *Lineality.* Coupled with the acceptance of hierarchical ordering of roles is the tendency either to be neutral about man's relationship to nature (Papajohn and Spiegel, 1975) or to feel that little can be done about the order of things (Looff, 1971).

The self-perception of children in each of these two classes are expected to differ structurally in the differential emphases of value themes shown in Table 2. We may speculate that lower-class children might perceive the self differently when they are with adults than when they are with children, a dif-

Table 2. Relative Position of Value Themes for the Middle Class and the Lower Class

Value	*Middle-Class Themes*	*Lower-Class Themes*
Activity	Doing → Being → Being-in-becoming	Being → Doing → Being-in-becoming
Relationship	Individuality → Collaterality → Lineality	Collaterality → Lineality → Individuality
Time	Future → Present → Past	Present → Past → Future
Man-Nature	Mastery → Subjugation → In harmony	Mastery → Subjugation → In harmony
Assistance	Competency → Compassion → Obligation	Compassion → Obligation → Competency

ference due to the lineality value. However, the middle-class child who has been socialized for individuality may hold the same self-perception with adults as with children. Such perceptual differences can form the bases of predicting structural differences in children's response to a self-concept or self-esteem instrument, as will be hypothesized below.

Ethnocultural Values Among the Lower Class

Differences among values of middle-class ethnocultures tend to become blurred. It is as if entrance into the dominant middle class in the United States were dependent upon holding shared cultural values (Werner and others, 1971). For example, Caudill and Frost found many similarities in the underlying value elements of the Tagakawa ethnic of the Japanese and the Puritan ethic. The similarities between these two value systems may be one of the reasons that the Japanese-American, of all the minority and different ethnocultures, have had the greatest success academically and economically (Caudill and Frost, 1975; Werner and others, 1971). The childrearing practices of the third-generation Japanese-American mother closely resemble those of the Caucasian mother (Caudill and Frost, 1975) and reflect those same values. Similarly, Schacter (1979) has found middle-class black mothers' childrearing practices in New York City to hold much more in common with practices of middle-class Caucasians than practices of lower-class blacks.

This assumption cannot be made about different ethnic groups of the lower class. The isolation of these groups into ghettos or rural areas tends to perpetuate unique ethnoculture value systems. Our direct experience has been with three lower-class ethnocultures, and we will limit our discussion to three groups: Puerto Rican, black, and anglo.

Each of these groups prizes the family or the extended kinship network. In each of these subcultures, the central focus of the network is likely to be a two-parent family (Cross, 1977; Looff, 1971; McAdoo, 1978; Papajohn and Spiegel, 1975; Ramirez and Castaneda, 1974). Love and joy have been reported to be the bases for relating the extended kinship networks in Puerto Rican (Ramirez and Castaneda, 1974) and black families (Cross, 1977; McAdoo, 1978). In contrast, Looff (1971) points out that the poor anglo living in Appalachia is bound to the family by obligation more than by caring and loving.

The value of the family implies collateral role relationships. Family interests are more important than individual interests, especially for Appalachian anglos and Puerto Ricans (Looff, 1971; Papajohn and Spiegel, 1975). Children in these families learn to value loyalty to the family in return for caregiving throughout life. The family provides an opportunity to express feelings and, for the very young, such expressions are seldom thwarted.

Although collaterality is valued, lineality is also important for Appalachian anglos and Puerto Ricans. Lineality is defined by sex and age relations, and deference is given to the male and to the oldest person (Matthews, 1965; Papajohn and Spiegel, 1975). Male dominance in decision making in the Puerto Rican family, however, appears to have been overemphasized. There is some evidence that the Puerto Rican female assumes an active role in decisions (Papajohn and Spiegel, 1975), perhaps more so than the Appalachian anglo female does (Matthews, 1965).

The collateral relations in the black family tend not to co-occur with an emphasis on lineality. There is mutual shared decision making between the male and the female (McAdoo, 1978), rather than the female dominance historically stipulated. The relationship between the individual and the family is one of loyalty and empathy. This relationship is most ascendant at times of crisis and ceremony. Although the extended family is valued, the nuclear family serves to establish individual identity (Cross, 1977).

Implications for Schooling

Our review has some interesting implications for schooling. The demands of the larger culture require children to adjust to the values of the dominant middle class. These are the values of compliance and diligence (Lortie, 1975). The pressures of adjustment to these demands will have a differential impact on the different subsets of children. For example, it has been noted extensively that success in school is measured by the child's adjustment to social demands and by learning how to read (Bowles and Gintis, 1976; Lortie, 1975).

In a pilot study in Atlantic City, New Jersey; Cleveland, Tennessee; and Polaski County, Arkansas, of lower-class anglo, black, and Puerto Rican boys and girls in first through third grades we found marked differences in how children constructed the self-concept, particularly in relation to academic achievement in learning to read. Our observations and work with the teachers confirmed that the school culture in all three settings, in all seven elementary schools, and in more than forty classrooms pressed these children toward the dual goals of behavioral control and learning to read.

Interesting patterns were found across ethnocultures. Black boys tended to associate ability to read with total evaluation of the self, whereas black girls associated reading with feelings about peers and teachers. Thus, the impact of the success or lack of success in the school culture has differential impact on the two sexes in the same ethnoculture. Black boys experienced more difficulty in learning to read than black girls and may have generalized the failure to the value of the self, whereas the black girls placed the ability to read in a social context of peers and teachers.

Puerto Rican boys and girls also differed. Puerto Rican boys associated reading with peers and evaluation of the self, whereas Puerto Rican girls associated reading with adult evaluations. To anglo boys of low socioeconomic status, reading was associated with the teacher's evaluation; to anglo girls, reading was grouped with notions of self-esteem. Thus, our pilot study revealed marked sex and ethnoculture differences as well as some similarities; the differences across sex and ethnoculture were much more striking than the similarities.

If one holds the currently popular assumption (Wittrock, 1979) that the teacher's major role in instruction is activating the child's interest in learning and instilling the desire to learn and that the stimulus for motivation is verbal reinforcement, then these differences are of critical importance to the teacher. Our sample suggests that the black male may be very responsive to information about his reading success, the black female may be motivated by personal feelings about peers and adults, the Puerto Rican male may respond to his interactions with other children, and Puerto Rican and anglo females may improve reading skills when their general self-esteem is heightened.

Finally, we should address the implications of these findings for school performance. The self-concept of children generally has been defined in terms of academic self-concept. In our pilot study we found that children who freely described the academic self included items that were not clearly academic. This finding suggests that, although school is a common experience, challenge to the self is defined according to cultural membership. Thus, in some cultures doing new things in conjunction with adults is an important self-structure, whereas in other cultures doing new things in the context of peers is important. The issue is how to help teachers tap a child's self-perception in a way that fosters academic growth.

Educators often view the self-concept of children as an opportunity for motivation (for instance, Sears, 1963). However, the generality that low academic performance is necessarily related to low self-concept may be erroneous. If a low self-concept is based on a qualitatively different self-concept than the qualitative difference provided, the teacher has an inaccurate base for using the self-concept as a motivational factor.

If the results of current studies of "teaching-learning" from a cognitive constructionist point of view are correctly interpreted, the major factor in the teacher's repertoire of skills is the identification and stimulation of a child's motivation to learn (Anastasiow and others, 1978; Wittrock, 1979). It is necessary in this theory for the teacher to assess accurately both the child's experiential background and the manner in which that experience has been organized. We believe that knowing how the child developed a value hierarchy and how the child organized the self-concept would be more useful tools for a teacher than trying to stimulate the child's learning activity.

Implications for Exceptionality

A quick survey of a series of reference books on exceptionality reveals that self-concept as a topic often is not included in the index. Most of the texts suggest ways one could improve self-concept of handicapped children, but rarely do these authors offer evidence that the self-concept of exceptional children is low. However, most authors make strong statements about the psychosocial difficulties handicapped children experience. For example, Lerner, Mardell-Czudnowski, and Goldberg (1981) conclude their chapter on psychosocial development as follows: "Handicapped children are likely to be rejected by parents, peers, and teachers, and disliked and ignored by others. Moreover, they are poor in perceiving social cues" (p. 224). These authors suggest a series of strategies, based on the work of Simon and O'Rourke, for developing stable and more positive feelings of self. Little research data are offered by the authors to support their claim. Kirk and Gallagher (1979), however, do offer research evidence that exceptional children have low self-concepts.

Kirk and Gallagher (1979) report a number of studies that suggest mentally retarded youngsters tend to have better self-concepts in special classes than retardates in regular classrooms. Kirk and Gallagher report similar findings for the deaf in regular and special school settings. Deaf youngsters attending residential schools tend to have better self-concepts than deaf children attending day schools. For both the educable retarded and the deaf, segregation by special disability tends to enhance their self-concepts. In spite of the current clamor of the dangers of labeling, Kirk and Gallagher believe the research evidence shows normal peers tend to reject the retarded and mentally ill because of their lack of academic skills and not because they are labeled.

There are two issues to be considered. First, too many youngsters from lower socioeconomic conditions are labeled as exceptional (Smith and Greenberg, 1975). Further, labeling as exceptional increases when a child is from a different ethnoculture and from the lower class (Mercer, 1973). We have pointed out that different value orientations are developed by children in the lower socioculture and minority ethnocultures; great care must be taken to prevent these very real value differences from being taken as exceptionality.

The second issue, in instances of well-diagnosed and documented handicaps, is the sorting out of the sociocultural and ethnocultural differences from the exceptionality. If children from the lower socioculture hold values markedly different from the values expected by the school, should we not also expect these differences among handicapped children from the lower socioculture and from different ethnocultures? A poor, black, and physically disabled child faces enormous obstacles, only some of which are based in the disability. That so many such children are able to surmount these obstacles is a testimony to the efforts of the child, the family, and teacher. That so many do not is a loss of valuable human energy.

At this time, with so little research evidence available, we can only speculate about the impact of lower socioculture and minority ethnoculture membership on the handicapped child. We believe that sociocultural and ethnocultural issues become blurred and that the "true" value differences held by these children are ascribed to their exceptionality rather than to what they have learned in their homes.

Also, parents of lower socioculture may value education but are less effective in teaching the skills related to IQ gains, verbal skills, and reading (Bradley and Caldwell, 1978; Schacter, 1979; Werner and Smith, 1977). Handicapped children who are both minority group members and reside in poverty will have less well-developed academic skills not due to their exceptionality but due to the teaching styles of their caregivers.

Recently, we saw a language-delayed, physically deformed child from a lower social class minority group in Hawaii. The child was physically deformed due to a brain insult. Her speech was delayed due to the nonverbalness of her home environment, which was also very accepting of her disability and non-motivating toward developmental gains or compensation for the disability. The child was not neglected in the negative sense of being ignored or uncared for, but neglected in that she was not provided the stimulation needed for normal development. This definition of neglect connotes value judgments derived from what is currently known about human development—and success in middle-class, white-dominated schools. This Hawaiian mother refused to accept that not talking to her child and not providing the necessary verbal stimulation further handicapped her child by the time she reached first grade. With great insight, she said, "Those are Haoli [anglo] and Japanese [Japanese-American] values—I don't want my child to be like that." Yet she desired her child to live well and do well as a human being and wanted her to do well in school, but as a noncompetitive human being.

These issues are difficult; we have no satisfactory answers and can only bring them to your attention. The self is a construction of each human being. Most of this self-construction is based on experiences specific to the individual. Self-esteem depends on the feedback each individual receives from attempts to understand and predict environmental events and the feedback each individual receives from the significant others in the environment. The success and value of those achievements is determined by others in the environment. The major thesis of this chapter is that sociocultural and ethnocultural differences lead to diverse notions of what an individual should achieve and how these achievements should be valued.

References

Anastasiow, N. J., Everett, M., O'Shaughnessey, T. E., Eggleston, P. J., and Eklund, S. J. "Using a Child Development Curriculum to Change Young Teenagers' Attitudes Toward Children, Handicapping Conditions and Hospital Settings." *American Journal of Orthopsychiatry,* 1978, *48* (4), 663–672.

Anderson, R. C., Spiro, R. J., and Montague, W. E. *Schooling and the Acquisition of Knowledge.* Hillsdale, N.J.: Erlbaum, 1977.

Attemborough, R. E., and Zdep, S. M. "Self-Image Among a National Probability Sample of Girls." *Proceedings of the 81st Annual Convention of the American Psychological Association,* Montreal, Canada, 1973, *8,* 237–238.

Bandura, A. "The Self-System in Reciprocal Determinism." *American Psychologist,* 1978, *33* (4), 344–358.

Bartlett, F. C. *Thinking.* New York: Basic Books, 1958.

Baumrind, D. "Socialization and Instrumental Competence in Young Children." In W. W. Hartup (Ed.), *The Young Child: Review of Research.* Vol. 2. Washington, D.C.: National Association for the Education of Young Children, 1972.

Berkowitz, L. *The Development of Motives and Values in the Child.* New York: Basic Books, 1964.

Bernstein, B. B. "A Critique of the Concept of Compensatory Education." In C. B. Cazden, V. P. John, and D. Hymes (Eds.), *Functions of Language in the Classroom.* New York: Teachers College Press, Columbia University, 1972.

Bowles, S., and Gintis, H. *Schooling in Capitalist America.* New York: Basic Books, 1976.

Bradley, R. H., and Caldwell, B. M. "Screening the Environment." *American Journal of Orthopsychiatry,* 1978, *48* (1), 114–130.

Caplin, M. D. "The Relationship Between Self-Concept and Academic Achievement." *The Journal of Experimental Education,* 1969, *37,* 13–16.

Carter, W. W. "Group Counseling for Adolescent Foster Children." *Children,* 1968, 15 (1), 22–27.

Caudill, W., and Frost, W. "A Comparison of Maternal Care and Infant Behavior in Japanese-American, American, and Japanese Families." In U. Bronfenbrenner and M. A. Mahoney (Eds.), *Influences on Human Development.* Hillsdale, N.J.: Erlbaum, 1975.

Cohen, S. *Social and Personality Development in Childhood.* New York: Macmillan, 1976.

Coopersmith, S. *The Antecedents of Self-Esteem.* San Francisco: W. H. Freeman, 1967.

Cross, W. E. "Black Family and Black Identity: A Literature Review." Paper presented at FCD Conference on Research Perspectives in the Ecology of Human Development, Cornell University, Ithaca, N.Y., 1977.

Elkind, D. *The Child's Reality: Three Developmental Themes.* Hillsdale, N.J.: Erlbaum, 1978.

Endler, N. S., and Magnusson, D. "Toward an Interactional Psychology of Personality." *Psychological Bulletin,* 1976, *83,* 956–974.

Epstein, H. T. "Phrenoblysis: Special Brain and Mind Growth Periods." Part 1, "Human Brain and Skull Development." Part 2, "Human Mental Development." *Developmental Psychobiology,* 1974, *7* (3), 207–224.

Fishbein, H. D. *Evolution, Development, and Children's Learning.* Santa Monica, Calif.: Goodyear, 1976.

Freedman, D. G. *Human Sociobiology.* New York: Free Press, 1979.

Gibson, E. J. *Principles of Perceptual Learning and Development.* New York: Appleton-Century-Crofts, 1969.

Goldschmidt, W. *Cultural Anthropology.* New York: American Library Association, 1967.

Hall, E. T. *Beyond Culture.* New York: Doubleday, 1976.

Healey, G. W., and DeBallasie, R. R. "A Comparison of Negro, Anglo, and Spanish American Adolescents' Self-Concepts." *Adolescence,* 1974, *9* (33), 15–24.

Hershovitz, M. J. *Cultural Relativism: Perspectives in Cultural Pluralism.* New York: Random House, 1973.

Hoffman, L. W. "The Father's Role in the Family and the Child's Peer-Group Adjustment." *Merrill-Palmer Quarterly,* 1961, *7,* 97–105.

Hoffman, L. W. "Early Childhood Experiences and Women's Achievement Motives." *Journal of Social Issues,* 1972, *28,* 129–155.

Jerison, H. J. "Paleoneurology and the Evolution of Mind." *Scientific American,* 1976, *234,* 64–79.

Kelly, G. A. *The Psychology of Personal Constructs.* New York: Norton, 1955.

Kerckhoff, A. C. *Socialization and Social Class.* Englewood Cliffs, N.J.: Prentice-Hall, 1972.

Kiefer, C. W. *Changing Cultures, Changing Lives: An Ethnographic Study of Three Generations of Japanese Americans.* San Francisco: Jossey-Bass, 1974.

Kirk, S. A., and Gallagher, J. J. *Educating Exceptional Children.* (3rd ed.) Boston: Houghton Mifflin, 1979.

Kluckhohn, R. *Culture and Behavior: Collected Essays of Clyde Kluckhohn.* New York: Free Press, 1962.

Lerner, J., Mardell-Czudnowski, C., and Goldberg, D. *Special Education for the Early Childhood Years.* Englewood Cliffs, N.J.: Prentice-Hall, 1981.

Loevinger, J. *Ego Development: Conceptions and Theories.* San Francisco: Jossey-Bass, 1976.

Looff, D. H. *Appalachia's Children: The Challenge of Mental Health.* Lexington: University Press of Kentucky, 1971.

Lortie, D. C. *School-Teacher: A Sociological Study.* Chicago: University of Chicago Press, 1975.

McAdoo, H. P. "Minority Families." In J. H. Stevens, Jr., and M. Matthews (Eds.), *Mother-Child, Father-Child Relationships.* Washington, D.C.: National Association for the Education of Young Children, 1978.

McClelland, D. C., Atkinson, J. W., Clark, R. A., and Lowell, E. L. *The Achievement Motive.* New York: Appleton-Century-Crofts, 1953.

Marx, R. W., and Winne, P. H. "Self-Concept and Achievement: Implications for Educational Programs." *Integrated Education,* 1975, *13,* 30–31.

Maslow, A. *Toward a Psychology of Being.* New York: Van Nostrand Reinhold, 1962.

Matthews, E. M. *Neighbor and Kin: Life in a Tennessee Ridge Community.* Nashville, Tenn.: Vanderbilt University Press, 1965.

Mead, G. H. *Mind, Self and Society.* Chicago: University of Chicago Press, 1934.

Mercer, J. R. *Labeling the Mentally Retarded.* Berkeley, Calif.: University of California Press, 1973.

Monge, R. H. "Developmental Trends in Factors of Adolescent Self-Concept." *Developmental Psychology,* 1973, *8* (3), 382–393.

Neisser, U. *Cognitive Psychology.* New York: Appleton-Century-Crofts, 1967.

Papajohn, J., and Speigel, J. *Transactions in Families: A Modern Approach for Resolving Cultural and Generational Conflicts.* San Francisco: Jossey-Bass, 1975.

Piaget, J. "Piaget's Theory." In P. H. Mussen (Ed.), *Carmichael's Manual of Child Psychology.* New York: Wiley, 1970.

Piaget, J., and Inhelder, B. *The Psychology of the Child.* New York: Basic Books, 1969.

Poppard, K. R., and Eccles, J. C. *The Self and Its Brain.* New York: Springer-Verlag, 1977.

Powers, J. M., Drane, H. T., Close, B. L., Noonan, M. P., Wineo, A. M., and Marshal, T. C. "A Research Note on the Self-Perception of Youth." *American Educational Research Journal,* 1971, *8* (4), 665–670.

Purkey, W. W. *Self-Concept and School Achievement.* Englewood Cliffs, N.J.: Prentice-Hall, 1970.

Ramirez, M., and Castaneda, A. *Cultural Democracy, Bi-Cognitive Development and Education.* New York: Academic Press, 1974.

Rodgers, C. R., and Dymond, R. F. *Psychotherapy and Personality Change.* Chicago: University of Chicago Press, 1954.

Rogers, C. M., Smith, M. D., and Coleman, J. M. "Social Comparison in the Classroom: The Relationship Between Academic Achievement and Self-Concept." *Journal of Educational Psychology,* 1978, *70,* 50–57.

Rokeach, M. *The Nature of Human Values.* New York: Free Press, 1973.

Rosenhan, D. "Prosocial Behavior of Children." In W. W. Hartey (Ed.), *The Young Child:*

Reviews of Research. Washington, D.C.: National Association for the Education of Young Children, 1972, *2,* 340–359.

Schachtel, E. G. *Metamorphosis.* New York: Basic Books, 1959.

Schacter, F. F. *Everyday Mother Talk to Toddlers: Early Intervention.* New York: Academic Press, 1979.

Schaffer, H. R. *Studies in Mother-Infant Interaction.* New York: Academic Press, 1977.

Sears, P. S. "The Effect of Classroom Conditions on the Strength of Achievement Motive and Work Output on Elementary School Children." United States Office of Education Cooperative Research Report, Project No. OE-873. Stanford, Calif.: Stanford University, 1963.

Sears, P. S., and Sherman, V. *In Pursuit of Self-Esteem.* Belmont, Calif.: Wadsworth, 1964.

Shavelson, R. J., Hubner, J. J., and Stanton, G. C. "'Self-Concept' Validation of Construct Interpretations." *Review of Educational Research,* 1976, *46* (3), 407–441.

Shipman, V. "Research Findings as Related to Educational Programming." In M. Scott and S. Grimmett (Eds.), *Current Issues in Child Development.* Washington, D.C.: National Association for the Education of Young Children, 1977, *2,* 49–60.

Smith, I., and Greenberg, S. "Teacher Attitudes and the Labeling Process." *Exceptional Children,* 1975, *41* (February), 319–324.

Soares, A. T., and Soares, L. "Self-Perceptions of Culturally Disadvantaged Children." *American Educational Research Journal,* 1969, *6,* 31–46.

Spitz, R. A. "Anaclitic Depression." *Psychoanalytic Study of Children,* 1946, *2,* 313–342.

Staub, E. "Socialization by Parents and Peers and Experiential Learning of Prosocial Behavior." In J. H. Steven, Jr., and M. Matthews (Eds.), *Mother-Child, Father-Child Relationships.* Washington, D.C.: National Association for the Education of Young Children, 1978.

Sullivan, H. S. *The Interpersonal Theory of Psychiatry.* New York: Norton, 1953.

Trowbridge, N. "Self-Concept and Socioeconomic Status in Elementary School Children." *American Educational Research Journal,* 1972, *9,* 525–538.

Tyler, L. E. *Individuality: Human Possibilities and Personal Choice in the Psychological Development of Men and Women.* San Francisco: Jossey-Bass, 1978.

Weinberg, M. *Minority Students: A Research Appraisal.* U.S. Department of Health, Education and Welfare, National Institute of Education, 1977.

Werner, E. E., Bierman, J. M., and French, F. E. *The Children of Kauai.* Honolulu: University Press of Hawaii, 1971.

Werner, E. E., and Smith, R. S. *Kauai's Children Come of Age.* Honolulu: University Press of Hawaii, 1977.

Werner, H. *Comparative Psychology of Mental Development.* (Rev. ed.) New York: International Universities Press, 1957.

Wittrock, M. C. "The Cognitive Movement in Instruction." *Educational Researcher,* 1979, *8* (2), 5–11.

Wober, M. "The Concept of Job Satisfaction Among Workers: In Particular, in a Nigerian Industry." *International Review of Applied Psychology,* 1971, *20* (1), 67–77.

Wylie, R. C. *The Self-Concept.* (Rev. ed.) Vol. I: *A Review of Methodological Considerations and Measuring Instruments.* Lincoln: University of Nebraska Press, 1975.

Nicholas J. Anastasiow is professor of psychiatry and associate director for research at the John F. Kennedy Child Development Center, University of Colorado Health Sciences Center.

Sadie Grimmett is associate professor of education and research associate at the Institute for Child Study, Indiana University.

Michael L. Hanes is professor of education and associate director for research in the School of Education, University of South Carolina.

The existence of a developmental handicap alters the attachment process
and has important implications for early emotional development.

Emotional Development
of the Young
Handicapped Child

Gordon Ulrey

The young child with a specific developmental disability is at increased risk for difficulties in other areas of development. For example, a motor deficit that decreases the child's activity level may reduce the child's opportunities for exploration of surroundings, thus reducing sensory experiences and learning. Abnormal motor movement may also make the child less "fun" to hold or cuddle, perhaps leading to less fondling and play time with caregivers. An apparently circumscribed disorder will affect the ecology of the child, altering many of the child's experiences and influencing parental attitudes, expectations, and behaviors. The emotional development of a young handicapped child must be understood in the context of how the disability has altered the child's experiences. Some children thrive emotionally against many odds and seem less vulnerable to the special risks of developmental disabilities. There is much to learn by a careful study of how young handicapped children develop emotionally.

Traditional assessments of school-age children delineate the child's deficits and may or may not describe specific competencies or capacities. For young handicapped children, this deficit model is often inadequate for diagnosing behavior disorders and for planning relevant intervention or educational programs. The past decade of research in early development indicates some important changes in emphasis and underscores the need for new applications of findings to existing models of assessment and intervention.

Four relevant issues have emerged in recent research with very young children (Yarrow, 1979):

1. The young child has a multitude of competencies that influence the behavior of the primary caregiver.
2. Early development is a function of a complex reciprocal interaction between the child and caregivers. The role of the child in eliciting responses from the caregiver and the attitudes and expectations of parents interact and change as the child matures.
3. The interdependence of cognitive and emotional development is important for understanding behavior and personality growth.
4. Understanding behavior in the context of the ecology of the child is necessary to determine the impact of existing handicaps.

The application of current child development research and analysis of the ecology of the child helps professionals appreciate two major points. One is that the young handicapped child may experience the world differently from nonhandicapped children; the second is that the handicapped child may experience additional stress, which can increase vulnerability to emotional deviance.

Impact of Handicaps on Interactions

Consideration of these two issues is an important step toward more relevant and valid assessments and toward more effective planning for interventions. The clinician and educator must attempt to understand the ecology of the handicapped child, since a valid assessment or appropriate treatment plan simply cannot be obtained without considering how the child's handicap influences his or her interactions with the environment and caregivers.

Insights from the Blind, Fraiberg's (1977) account of ten otherwise normal blind children, is a model of what can be learned by considering how differently a handicapped child may experience the world and the impact this difference may have on the primary caregiver and upon the child's emotional development. The blind child is less able to produce important behaviors such as eye contact, often has a muted or delayed smile response, and exhibits delayed discrimination and recognition of the caregiver—thus greatly increasing the risk of altering or delaying the formation of an attachment with the primary caregiver. A poor early attachment may compromise all subsequent emotional development and the capacity to relate to others (Bowlby, 1969). Fraiberg's insights have resulted from her careful study of how interactions with the environment are altered or disrupted because of a child's handicap. She demonstrates that much can be learned from the study of the effect of abnormalities on the emotional development of children.

Several longitudinal studies have attempted to determine which factor or factors in early development predict later emotional and behavior disorders. Reviews of the major longitudinal studies conclude that there simply are no known consistent single behavioral indicators of later emotional disorders present in the first two years of life (Sameroff, 1976; Beckwith, 1979). The limited prediction of single factors is seen most dramatically in the fact that some children with multiple risk factors develop later emotional functioning. Sameroff (1976) suggests the problem is that most longitudinal studies assume that single variables or events in a child's life have a linear causality to later disabilities. A remarkable exception is the longitudinal study by Werner and others (1971) of children in Kauai. This study reported and compared both child factors (biological and psychological data) and environmental factors (sociecomomic levels, family stability, and so on). The consideration of both types of risk factors, as well as interactions between the child and caregivers, increased prediction of later behavior and learning problems.

Impressed with the Kauai study, Sameroff (1976) argues for the importance of considering the interactions of "transactions" that occur between the child and environment. Study of human interactions requires a more complex model of development—a model that not only sees the child responding to the environment but also stresses the reciprocal effect of the child on the environment. A linear model focused on single variables is seen as too simplistic to explain the complexity of emotional development. Sameroff argues that "only when development is appreciated as a complex interplay between the child's changing competencies and temperament and the changing attitude and behavior of the important socializing agents in the environment can the prediction problem be squarely faced" (p. 147). This transactive model is not only needed for accurate prediction, but it is also needed for understanding the dynamics of emotional development of the handicapped child. Thus, the professional must examine how a handicap of a nonemotional base may affect the risks for emotional and behavior disorders.

Children with a wide range of handicaps are found to have a higher incidence of emotional and behavioral problems than their nonaffected peers. Recent findings indicate an increased incidence of behavioral disorders among children with such handicaps as minimal brain dysfunction (Graham and others, 1968), mild mental retardation (Chess and Hassibi, 1970), hearing impairment (Schlesinger and Meadow, 1972), or visual impairment (Fraiberg and others, 1969). Thomas and Chess (1977) conclude from several longitudinal studies of handicapped children that the presence of a disability increases the stress of accomplishing normal developmental tasks. That is, sensory impairment and physical disorders may impede or interfere with emotional development but are not necessarily the cause. There are important insights professionals can gain by carefully examining the ecology of the young handicapped child. These insights will help both in evaluating developmental disorders and in planning interventions.

The theoretical framework of attachment-separation-individuation will be described as the developmental process for the formation of human relationships, which begin with the child and important caregivers. This framework will enable the clinician to understand better the impact of a disorder on emotional development. Because establishment of a primary relationship is seen as the foundation for future human relations throughout life, the impact of specific disorders on early emotional development will be described; and implications for preventions, assessment, and educational planning will be discussed.

Concepts of Vulnerability and Coping

It is clear that the young handicapped child is generally more vulnerable to developing behavior problems and to experiencing stress when attempting to cope with the problems of daily living. In attempting to understand why, studies of "wellness" (the successful process of coping and adapting) offer a positive orientation to helping children at increased risk for problems. For example, Murphy (1976) reports the results of a longitudinal study of middleclass children in Kansas and reviews general characteristics of children and families that are successfully coping and adapting to stress. Anthony (1974) has introduced the concept of an invulnerability syndrome, which is associated with the coexistence of high-risk factors and low vulnerability. The study of children who survive substantial risk, such as a psychotic parent, provides insights into what makes children more vulnerable or less so (Anthony, 1974; Garmezy and Nuechterlein, 1972; Pines, 1979). The resiliency of children who survive multiple risks has been described by Sameroff and Chandler (1975) as a self-righting tendency. In this view, the child is seen as able to elicit support and resources in the face of stress and to stay on course toward healthy emotional development. Supporting this view is Goldberg's (1977) finding that a critical factor appears to be the infant's competence in eliciting attention and care from the environment.

Werner and Smith (1981) have reviewed current studies of vulnerability and invulnerablity and report data on a longitudinal study of a subgroup of 72 children in Kauai, selected from a cohort of 693. Their study compared children categorized as at high risk for behavior disorders who did not show problems at eighteen years of age (invulnerable) with a matched group of high-risk children who did develop problems (vulnerable). They found the following characteristics of young children who were described as invulnerable:

1. More were first-born males.
2. Few of the children had congenital defects or CNS damage.
3. They were socially responsive and energetic (temperament).
4. They were able to elicit attention from caregivers.
5. They had a "good" genetic background (that is, their family histories showed few mental health problems.)
6. They had autonomous personality patterns.

Werner and Smith also noted the characteristics of families in which high-risk children were found to be invulnerable. They were:

1. At least one caregiver in the environment was stable.
2. Other caregivers (father, older sibling, grandparents) were available.
3. There were few chronic illnesses and low total stress factors.
4. A primary caretaker was available.

The studies reviewed by Werner and Smith indicate in general that the invulnerable child developed a strong early attachment and autonomy during the preschool years, mastered competencies in childhood, and had a sense of some control over life events during adolescence. The home environment had at least one stable caregiver (a parent, sibling, or grandparent) who was supportive but not overprotective and who fostered the child's growing autonomy. These appear to be necessary factors that contribute to healthy emotional development when the risks for vulnerability are high. More research is needed to learn how behavior characteristics of high-risk children interact with specific environmental risk factors. For example, sex differences, birth rank, cultural difference, and socioeconomic status are all factors related to vulnerability, but they are interrelated in ways not yet fully understood.

The study of vulnerability and invulnerability provides useful information for professionals about what factors may help individual children survive increased stress and other risk factors. This information should assist professionals in counseling parents of handicapped children. Vulnerablity and coping relate directly to early emotional development. A fact that emerges clearly from the research is that basic autonomy and competence are formed in infancy through the child-caregiver attachment system. Next we will examine how attachment is accomplished.

Attachment

The role of attachment in early emotional development has been emphasized as a critical phenomenon by several investigators (Ainsworth, 1973; Bowlby, 1969; Yarrow and others, 1972). It is assumed that to develop ego functions and master later tasks of emotional development, the infant must form an attachment with a primary caretaker (Spitz, 1965). That is, the child must first attach before psychological birth or the process of separation and individuation can occur (Mahler, 1972). Sroufe and Waters (1976) conceptualize attachment as a developmental/organizing construct that must be understood as a constellation of enduring behaviors rather than a static trait. However, some investigators (Weinraub and others, 1977) disagree. They argue that the attachment construct as a qualitatively different relationship between the child and caregiver is of limited value and instead describe attachment as a behavioral trait. If attachment is considered from a developmental, interactive model (Sroufe, 1979), the emphasis shifts to attachment as a persistent affective bond between the young child and caregiver. In this model, attachment is seen as a function of cognitive and affective development and can be understood only as a complex interaction of the maturation of these factors and environmental events.

One important implication of the developmental interactive viewpoint (Sroufe, 1979) is that attachment is conceptualized as an affective bond; thus, differences in quality of attachment will occur. Differences in child and caregiver interactions will influence the degree of attachment and later emotional development of the child. Yarrow and others (1972) report that differences in the quality of attachment have been linked to the quality of later attachments and relationships. Formation of the affective bond results from the complex and subtle process of interactions between the child and caretaker; examining the process may reveal why handicapped children may be more vulnerable than normal children to later emotional disorders. Although there are few if any factors in early development that predict later emotional problems (Beckwith, 1979), there are numerous implications for helping parents cope as well as for facilitating the emotional adaptation of the child and caregivers (Solnit and Provence, 1979).

Investigators of the attachment process have been impressed with the degree of interdependence of cognitive, affective, and motivational aspects of infant behavior. For example, the formation of a good attachment depends on the infant eliciting behaviors from the caregiver and reciprocal responses from the environment. Attachment studies reveal that the infants' visual discrimination (recognition of the caregiver), activity level (degree of responsiveness), and smiling behavior are essential for obtaining optimal responses from the caregiver. Conversely, the consistency and quality of response from the caregiver also influences the endurance of these attachment-producing behaviors. The child with abnormalities that result in decreased potential for eliciting these behaviors from the caregiver may be more vulnerable to later behavior problems. Of course, in such a case, the attitudes, expectations, and stability of the family are also determinant variables. For example, the visually handicapped child may not show the expected recognition and smiling behaviors (Fraiberg and others, 1969), and the motor-handicapped child may be more active or less so (Prechtel, 1963). Parents' understanding of their own needs and expectations and their abilities to adapt to the special circumstances are critical if a quality affective bond is to be formed.

Ainsworth (1973) describes the attachment process of normal children as progressing through four phases and requiring from ten to twelve months. During the first phase, the child indicates a discrimination of a primary caregiver, usually by smiling. The second phase consists of a differential response to the caregiver during a time of stress, usually crying followed by comforting by the caregiver. In the third phase, the child initiates contact with the caregiver by crawling or reaching specifically to her or him. During the fourth phase, stranger anxiety emerges; the child shows strong preference for the primary caregiver and demonstrates a fear of strangers and separation from the caregiver.

As the child forms an affective bond, he or she begins what Mahler and others (1975) describe as psychological birth, in which the child separates from the caregiver and begins to function with increased autonomy. The separation process overlaps with attachment and occurs approximately between the ages of three months and three years. Mahler describes this phase of emotional development as separation and individuation and sees it as the basis for all future emotional health (Mahler and others, 1975).

Separation and Individuation

During the first three or four months of life, the primary caretaker (usually the mother) meets the child's basic needs. The child begins to associate with the mother the pleasure of having needs met; this pleasure strengthens the attachment bond. The affective bond must occur if the child is to begin slowly to grow psychologically and physically away from dependence on the caretaker. As the child learns to differentiate the caretaker from others and responds accordingly, he or she begins the slow process of moving away from total dependence. The child's specific smile response to the caretaker (two to three months) and fear reaction to strangers (eight to ten months) are not only milestones of the attachment process but also signs of the discrimination needed for separation and individuation from the primary caretaker.

As has been noted, the separation process begins when the child differentiates himself or herself from the primary caretaker. Later, the child's cognitive, emotional, and motor maturation makes increased movement away from the caretaker possible. Having developed the capacity for reaching, the child can then periodically return to the caregiver for what Mahler and others (1975) call "emotional refueling." The successful mastering of separation results in the child's autonomous functioning, although he or she continues to need some closeness to the caregiver.

The individuation process requires that the child internalize both a cognitive and affective sense of the caregiver. The child who successfully individuates has a mental image of the parent and only occasionally needs to see the caregiver. Mahler describes the image as object constancy, which implies that the child is satisfied both that the caretaker exists when not seen and that emotional support will be provided if necessary.

Mahler and others (1975) describe four subphases of the separation-individuation process:

1. **Differentiation (five to ten months).** The child begins to discriminate differences in people and the environment and explores the world by sight and reaching. Cognitive maturity and increased motor skills for exploration and movement (crawling) allow the child to move from close physical contact with the caregivers.

2. **Practice (ten to fifteen months).** The child normally learns to walk; greatly expanded exploration is done with excitement and enthusiasm. The child now returns periodically to the caregiver for emotional refueling and reassurance that the caregiver is there and dependable.

3. **Rapprochement (fifteen to twenty-five months).** The child now expands exploration and movement away from the caregiver but at the same time becomes more aware of his or her helplessness and dependence. This results in ambivalence with more extremes of alternate closeness to and rejection of the caregiver (for example, saying "no," and temper tantrums of the two-year-old). The child's ambivalence and what appears to be regression is seen as communication. Although words are used in this phase, the frustrated use of gestures when the child is not understood is also seen.

4. **Partial Object Constancy (twenty-four to thirty-six months).** The image of the caregiver is now internalized and the child can function independently. Because the child is struggling for autonomy, there is some conflict when parents make demands. While the child is working through the conflict of limits placed by parents and his or her own striving for independence, the child is also aware of his or her helplessness and dependence on the parent.

The separation and individuation phase of early emotional development overlaps with and is seen as an extension of the attachment process. The attachment-separation-individuation (ASI) process provides a conceptual framework and observable developmental milestone. The factors that influence ASI can be understood only as a complex system. The clinician should be aware that abnormalities in any part of the process, such as in parental attitudes or in the child's behavior, will change the system.

Impact of Handicaps on ASI

Although attachment occurs in almost all cases except cases of early infantile autism (Kenner, 1943), there are important differences in the quality of attachment (Sroufe, 1979). When a poor attachment occurs, the subsequent development of human relationships may be compromised. The presence of a developmental handicap represents a significant stress on the process of ASI — it increases the vulnerablity of both the child and caregivers.

There has been little research on the impact of specific handicaps on ASI behaviors and later emotional development. However, there is an increase in information about the impact of various characteristics of infants, caregivers, and interactions that influence early child caretaker interactions. These characteristics have been recently reviewed by Osofsky and Connors (1979). Stone and Chesney (1979) conducted a study of fifteen infants in an intervention program. The infants demonstrated a variety of handicaps and all showed disturbances in one or more attachment behaviors. Stone and Chesney hypothesize that impairments in the infants' expression of affective states make it more difficult for caregivers to receive and understand the child's signals. The authors stress the need for research to determine the impact of various handicaps on the attachment process and to facilitate anticipating guidance and intervention.

The implication of viewing the ASI process as a system is that any significant change or event will produce disequilibrium; some assimilation, accommodation, and adaptation will be required to restore equilibrium. The presence of a handicap is just such a significant event, and it will alter the system in some way. The process is complex because changes in one area will influence other areas. For example, the mother of a handicapped infant may feel rejected by her child's passivity (temperament) or actual deficit (decreased muscle tone). She may subsequently be unable to respond with the extra patience and sacrifice needed to form a strong affective bond with the child. Based on what is currently known about factors influencing the ASI process and relationships between young children and caregivers, some implications can be drawn for various handicaps, as follows:

Motor Deficits. The importance of early physical contact between neonates and mothers has been emphasized by several authors (Klaus and Kennell, 1976; Wolff, 1959). Kennell and others (1974) report that mothers who were allowed physical contact with their nude baby — for one hour in the first two hours after delivery and an extra five hours each day for the next three days — showed increased later contact. When compared to a matched control group (routine neonatal care involved less physical contact) two years later, mothers exposed to early physical contact showed significantly more later physical contact, more vocalization, and more eye contact with their children while they underwent a stressful physical exam. The authors concluded that physical contact is important to facilitate the development of a child's attachment with the primary caregiver. Recognition of the importance of early physical contact has resulted in a number of changes in neonatal care (Wolff, 1959). The Brazelton Neonatal Behavioral Scale (Brazelton, 1973) is now frequently used to help parents develop individualized approaches to facilitate reciprocal interactions (Erickson, 1976).

Clinicians may question the extent to which newborns with a motor deficit experience early interactions with caregivers differently from nonafflicted newborns. Prechtel (1963) observed a group of infants with minimal brain dysfunction who had abnormal muscle tone (hypertonia). These babies were not able to relax when handled by their mothers and seemed to have difficulty molding to their mothers. In a study of motor disorders of infants and young children, Molnar (1978) reports that a significant number of mentally retarded young children show delays in postural adjustments to caregivers. Children with motor deficits (such as abnormal muscle tone or persistent primitive reflexes) may be at increased risk because the early physical handling of these infants may make parents feel rejected or inadequate. If the child is not able to adjust to the physical comforting offered by the parent, there is an increased risk of the parent minimizing physical contact.

There is also evidence that subtle but important communications, which are dependent on motor movements, take place between the infant and caregiver. Condon and Sanders (1974) report that normal infants develop complex synchronized motor movements in response to to parental voice and physical contact. They postulate that achieving such a synchronous interaction is important for future child and caretaker interactions and communication. Infants with abnormal motor skills may take longer to respond in a synchronous manner or may not be able to respond in such a manner at all.

Abnormal muscle tone may also influence a child's activity level and facial movements. These are important because they provide cues from which the mother determines her emotional responses (Bennett, 1971). Children with cerebral palsy often have delayed expressive language. This delay also decreases the child's potential for interacting with or eliciting positive responses from the parent (de Hirsch, 1973). The subtle decreases in a child's emotional expressions caused by a motor deficit require special adaptations by parents if quality attachment is to occur. When parents are unable to help the child compensate, or when parents feel rejected and withdraw, the child becomes more vulnerable to the formation of a compromised or limited attachment with the caregivers.

Motor deficits or delays may also disrupt the ASI process if they limit a child's movements away from the caregiver. Behavior such as reaching, crawling, and walking enables the child to separate from the caregiver and develop autonomy. The prolonged dependence of the child may stress the parent as well.

Many parents are able to make the sacrifices and adjustments needed to form a healthy relationship with a child who has a motor handicap. When the child and/or parents are vulnerable, there are several things professionals can do to help. Accurate assessment of the child's motor skills and of the parent-child relationship can be used to plan intervention or anticipate guidance. For example, physical therapy techniques (Bobath, 1977) can be used to alter the child's muscle tone and encourage mutual cuddling. However, the clinician should be aware that programs that provide intensive motor therapy without involving parents may further delay the development of ASI.

Visual Handicaps. As indicated above, the one handicap area that has been studied for its impact on emotional development is visual impairment.

Because many of the signals of communication and indication of emotion between infants and caregivers are visual, the importance of vision in the ASI process is obvious. Within several hours after birth, normally sighted infants show preference for a familiar face rather than for nonfamiliar stimuli (Goren, 1975). The normal child's recognition of the caregiver and discrimination of strangers are also primarily mediated by vision. In contrast, the early development of psychotic children indicates relative lack of eye contact and increased aversion to gazing at the human face. Blind children may not form a strong attachment because of decreased interaction with caregivers. This lack may compromise future human relationships unless alternative modalities can be used to process external cues for interactions.

There is an increased risk that the affective bond of attachment will be disrupted or will not occur for blind children (Fraiberg, 1971). In her longitudinal study of ten otherwise normal children, Fraiberg (1975) emphasizes that the blind child's major task during early infancy is to form a quality attachment with the caregiver. There are several reasons the blind child is less able to elicit positive responses from the caregiver during early infancy. Smiling and recognition of the caregiver do develop in blind children, but they are altered by the lack of visual feedback; the smile is often muted and delayed (Fraiberg, 1968). The recognition of caregivers and discrimination of strangers is also delayed for blind children (Adelson and Fraiberg, 1973). Between the ages of ten and eighteen months, blind children begin to show anxiety at the presence of strangers; normally sighted children do so between eight and fourteen months. Other modalities—such as tactile and auditory—can be substituted for the visual to help blind children form early relationships. However, development of these modalities requires adaptation by parents, and attachment still will be delayed.

The fact that blind children show 25 percent higher incidence of emotional and behavior disorders than sighted children suggests they experience increased stress in their emotional development. These stresses can be reduced if parents are helped to form an appropriate relationship with the blind child and if they are taught the ways the child can learn to use other senses to mediate recognition of caregivers and discrimination of strangers. The parents must be informed that later separation and individuation may also be delayed because of the child's dependence on close proximity to caregivers.

Hearing Loss. The ASI process is mediated in important ways by vocalization of the child and caregiver (Ainsworth, 1973). There is evidence of early discrimination of sounds that influence interactions. For example, mothers are able to differentiate crying responses indicating pleasure, recognition, hunger, or fear within the first month of a child's life (Wolff, 1971). An infant demonstrates differential responses to the mother's voice and the voice of a stranger as early as two weeks of age (Hammond, 1970). As noted above, Condon and Sanders (1974) have observed synchronized motor movement responses to vocalization. Clearly, the recognition and discriminating of vocalization interact in a complex and important way to influence the early relationship between the child and caregiver.

The child with impaired hearing or intermittent hearing loss secondary to infection (otitis media) may be at increased risk for disruption of the attachment process. Children need early screening for hearing deficits and careful monitoring if they have an intermittent hearing loss. Parents need counseling so that potential disruptions can be avoided.

Because a hearing impairment will also delay verbal skills, the deaf child's limited verbal language may also delay separation and individuation. The development of autonomy normally begins with the child's spoken word *no* and the child's testing of limits. When the process occurs without spoken words, it is difficult for the child to express needs and for the parent to understand them. Toddlers with delayed verbal skills may become locked into a behavior struggle with parents because the child may be able to get attention only by being disruptive behaviorally (Schlesinger, 1978).

Other Developmental Delays. The special problems in the emotional development of mentally retarded children (Zigler and Harter, 1969) and children with physical disabilities (Richardson, 1969) have been described by other authors. While developmental handicaps affect the entire socialization process, there may be specific adverse influences on early emotional development. For example, the above authors stress the need to focus on the feelings and behaviors of parents of very young handicapped children. How parents feel about having a disabled child and what they believe other people think about their child will influence early parent-child interactions.

Children who remain in families show significantly greater intellectual and emotional functioning than children who are placed in institutions (Koch and de la Cruz, 1975). In general, delayed milestones of development decrease the infant's potential for eliciting responses from caregivers (Stone and Chesney, 1979). When the appearance of the smile response is delayed or recognition and discrimination of caregivers and strangers are delayed, the parents must make an extra effort to maintain the interactions necessary for achieving a strong attachment. Counseling of parents of premature infants or children identified early as developmentally delayed (for instance, children with Down's syndrome) can facilitate the interactions between the child and caregiver.

One other point should be clear to the professional and parents: The early identification of infants who have experienced high-risk events (for instance, prematurity or anoxia at birth) may have inadvertent effects on parents. Kearsley (1979) argues for possible iatrogenic causes of mental retardation in which focus on the "sick" child may cause parents to withdraw and to lower their expectations for and investment in a child. When an infant is identified as handicapped, the professionals must consider the vulnerability of parents and families and must plan intervention that acknowledges the feelings and behaviors of caregivers. The parents' anxiety about having a "defective" child may make it difficult for them to interact appropriately with the child and provide necessary stimulation. There is always a need for counseling follow-up with parents who are told their child is at risk. This counseling helps avoid a disruption of the formation of a quality attachment and the development of autonomy in the identified child.

Attitudes and Expectations of Caregivers

The impact of a handicap on an infant can be understood only in terms of the expectations and the changing attitudes of the parents. Anthony and Benedek (1970) describe the process by which parents prepare themselves for parenthood and the adjustments that must occur subsequent to the birth. The psychological preparation for the birth of a child involves fantasizing about the idealized child (preferred sex, temperament, size, and so on) and the feared child (defective, weak, passive, or tyrannical and difficult to control). The parents must work through discrepancies between the imagined child and the reality of the actual child. When a child is perceived as being defective or as having a difficult temperament, working through feelings elicited by the child and feelings of loss of the idealized child make parents more vulnerable. This vulnerability in turn increases the risk that they may form an attachment of poor quality with the child.

The birth of a handicapped child introduces a significant stress to a family system; indeed, some researchers report an increase of marital discord and divorce (Bloom and others, 1978) when a handicapped child is born. The vulnerability of the mother may escalate because of postpartum depression or marital discord, which makes it even more difficult for her to respond to the child's extraordinary needs. When the child is limited in capacity to elicit responses from caregivers, the risk increases. The combination of factors may lead to the vicious circle of feelings of rejection and avoidance, which contribute to a poor attachment.

Osofsky and Connors (1979) and Parke (1979) review the importance of numerous parental characteristics, attitudes, and expectations to the early relationships between infants with caregivers. The reviewers cite a wide variety of child characteristics, parent characteristics, and environmental factors that relate to child and caretaker interactions. The parent–child interaction process is vastly more complex than has been appreciated in the past. There is little use in isolating child or parent behaviors outside the context of the interaction. One important area is the differences that relate to socioeconomic status. For example, Messer and Lewis (1972) report that middle-class mothers, observed when their children were two years old, verbalized with their toddlers seven times more frequently than comparable lower-class mothers. Cultural differences have also been found. For example, American mothers use more face-to-face or visual contact and less physical contact than non-American Oriental mothers (Goldberg, 1977). To be effective, counseling parents of handicapped children must take into account cultural and socioeconomic factors.

Parents adjusting to having a handicapped child may go through a process analogous to grieving (Solnit and Stark, 1961). The parents may experience as loss the awareness of a child's deficit or the discrepancy between the idealized child and the actual child. For example, when the parent expects a warm, cuddling child and the child is overactive and aloof, the parent must resolve the loss of the expected responses of the child. The clinician must therefore study the compatibility between parents and infants if he or she is to intervene and effectively help parents adapt.

Goodness of Fit

Studies of differences in the temperament of children have led to insights into how behavioral characteristics of children affect interaction with caregivers. Thomas and others (1968) investigated ten different behavior categories that relate to temperament (activity level, rhythmicity, approach–withdrawal, adaptability, intensity of reactions, threshold responsiveness, quality of mood, distractability, attention span, and persistence). Temperament behaviors are found to cluster in three different groups described as (1) easy, (2) difficult, and (3) slow to warm up. A scale developed by Carey (1972) makes it possible to assess the temperament of infants and young children. Such measurement of temperament has made it possible to examine the impact of different styles of parenting on children with different temperaments. Thomas and Chess (1977) stress the fact that measurements of temperament are only meaningful when considered in the context of the child's environment.

"Goodness of fit" is defined as the degree of consonance or dissonance between the child and parent. A fit is consonant when the properties of the environment and the parent's expectations and demands are in accord with the child's capacities, characteristics, and styles of behaving. Dissonance occurs when environmental opportunity and parental demands are discrepant with the capacities and characteristics of the child. The goodness of fit is always relative to attitudes, expectations of parents, and the demands of a given culture (or socioeconomic pressures). In theory, a consonant fit leads to optimal development of the child.

The goodness of fit provides a model for intervention with the vulnerable or at-risk family with a handicapped child. The specific area of child interaction can be identified along with the temperamental style of the child and parental behaviors that contribute to dissonance in the family system. Specific parental attitudes and practices that may interfere with the child's optimal development may be identified and modified. This process helps the clinician plan intervention strategies to minimize the dissonance. It is important that the parent not be viewed as a "bad" or "good" parent, but merely as a parent who needs help to find a more adaptive way of responding to the child's constellation of behaviors. At times work is needed to help the parent appreciate and accept deficits in the child (for example, working through the grief of losing the idealized child).

Conclusion

A conceptual framework of early emotional development through the ASI process has been described. There has been a discussion of a complex model for understanding the reciprocity and changes that result in the interaction between a child and his or her caregivers. The fact that an increased incidence of later emotional and behavioral problems occur for handicapped children suggests that a handicap increases the stress for mastering tasks of emotional development. Several specific (although complex and overlapping) effects of handicaps on the ASI process have been discussed. An appreciation of how specific deficits may influence the ecology of an individual child's family environment is necessary for the clinician and educator to understand the emotional development of young handicapped children. The interactive model provides a framework from which professionals can plan relevant and reliable assessment, anticipatory guidance, and intervention programs.

Several important implications for prevention, assessment, and intervention are based on clinical practices and research findings reviewed above. For prevention, risk or vulnerability factors in the child and environment must be determined. Parent counseling and specific techniques can be used to minimize the stress on the family and handicapped child, but intervention must occur during early infancy. A cautionary note is that parents must not be made to feel guilty if they have difficulty attaching to a severely handicapped child or effecting significant changes. The clinician should not imply that if parents can only be "good," the child will be fine. Instead, the child's impact on the caregiver must be considered as must the goodness of fit between caregivers and the child.

When assessing young children, the clinician must observe parent–child interactions, as well as characteristics of the child and parents, that may make forming relationships more difficult. In addition to traditional psychological tests, clinicians have at their disposal several scales that provide relevant assessment data. These scales measure attachment (Ainsworth, 1973), temperament (Carey, 1972), separation and individuation (Mosey and others, 1980), and self-help skills (Doll, 1965). The need for professionals to expand procedures for assessing young handicapped children has been stressed by Simenson and others (1980). Expanded scales and observations of interactions

48

provide valuable information about the ecology of the child and the child's level of emotional development, information which is not obtained from traditional cognitive measures.

When the child's level of ASI is considered, clinicians may find some traditional techniques for treatment inappropriate. For example, when the child has temper tantrums, ignoring the child and using time-out procedures may not always be appropriate. If the child is emotionally immature, he or she may need emotional refueling from a caretaker; in such a case, physical contact and reassurance may be most appropriate. Isolating a child during the separation and individuation period actually may increase the stress on the child and delay emotional development. The caretaker must be involved in early intervention since developmentally delayed, handicapped children and their parents may need help learning adaptive interactive patterns. Placing very young handicapped children in programs without caretakers for a full day may prolong emotional development (Mordock, 1979); the young child may benefit more from interactions with caregivers during which ASI is completed and the stress of emotional development is reduced.

There is a need for research to determine the effectiveness of helping caretakers interact with a handicapped child and research that explores which intervention procedures are most appropriate in given cases. As professionals come to better understand how handicapped children develop emotionally and how they experience the world differently, we will be better prepared to decrease vulnerability and risk factors. Segal and Yahraes (1978) describe helping children learn how to cope as producing "children who will not break." As we have seen, it may be much more difficult to achieve this state with sensory-impaired children, but it is possible once teachers and parents are more aware of how children develop and how to compensate for deficits.

References

Adelson, E., and Fraiberg, S., "Gross Motor Development in Infants Blind from Birth." *Child Development,* 1973, *45,* 114–126.
Ainsworth, M. S. "The Development of Infant–Mother Attachment." In B. Caldwell and H. Ricciuti (Eds.), *Review of Child Development Research.* Vol. 3. Chicago: University of Chicago Press, 1973.
Anthony, E. J. "Introduction: The Syndrome of the Psychologically Vulnerable Child." In E. J. Anthony and L. Koupernick (Eds.), *The Child in His Family and Children at Psychiatric Risk.* New York: Wiley, 1974.
Anthony, E. J., and Benedek, T. (Eds.). *Parenthood and Psychology and Psychopathology.* Boston: Little, Brown, 1970.
Beckwith, L. "Prediction of Emotional and Social Behavior." In J. Osofsky (Ed.), *Handbook of Infant Development.* New York: Wiley, 1979.
Bennett, S. "Infant–Caretaker Interactions." *Journal of the American Academy of Child Psychiatry,* 1971, *10,* 321–335.

Bloom, B. L., Asher, S. J., and White, S. W. "Marital Disruption as a Stressor: A Review and Analysis." *Psychological Bulletin*, 1978, *85*, 867–894.

Bobath, B. *Abnormal Postural Reflex Activity Caused by Brain Lesions.* New York: Heineman, 1977.

Bowlby, J. *Attachment and Loss.* Vols. 1 and 2. New York: Basic Books, 1969.

Brazelton, T. B. "Neonatal Behavioral Assessment Scale." *Clinics in Developmental Medicine*, no. 50. Philadelphia: Lippincott, 1973.

Carey, W. B. "Clinical Application of Infant Temperament Measurement." *Journal of Pediatrics*, 1972, *81*, 823–828.

Chess, S., and Hassibi, M. "Behavior Deviations in Mentally Retarded Children." *Journal of American Academy of Child Psychiatry*, 1970, *9*, 282–297.

Condon, W., and Sanders, L. "Neonatal Movement Is Synchronized with Adult Speech: Interactional Participation in Language Acquisition." *Science*, 1974, *183*, 99–101.

de Hirsch, K. "Early Language Development and Minimal Brain Dysfunction." In F. de la Cruz, B. Fox, and H. Roberts (Eds.), *Minimal Brain Dysfunction, Annals of the New York Academy of Sciences*, 1973, *205*, 158–163.

Doll, E. *Vineland Social Maturity Scale.* Circle Pines, Minn.: American Guidance Service, 1965.

Erickson, M. L. *Assessment and Management of Developmental Changes in Children.* St. Louis, Mo.: Mosby, 1976.

Fraiberg, S. "Parallel and Divergent Patterns in Blind and Sighted Infants." *Psychoanalytic Study of the Child*, 1968, *23*, 264–299.

Fraiberg, S. "Interaction in Infancy: A Program for Blind Infants." *Journal of the American Academy of Child Psychiatry*, 1971, *10* (3), 381–408.

Fraiberg, S. "The Development of Human Attachment in Infants Blind from Birth." *Merrill-Palmer Quarterly*, 1975, *21*, 315–334.

Fraiberg, S. *Insights from the Blind.* New York: Basic Books, 1977.

Fraiberg, S., Smith, M., and Adelson, E. "An Education Program for Blind Infants." *The Journal of Special Education*, 1969, *3* (2), 121–139.

Garmezy, N., and Nuechterlein, K. "Vulnerability and Invulnerable Children: The Fact and Fiction of Competence and Disadvantage." *American Journal of Orthopsychiatry*, 1972, *77* (abstract).

Goldberg, S. "Social Competence in Infancy: A Model of Parent–Infant Interaction." *Merrill-Palmer Quarterly*, 1977, *23*, 163–177.

Goren, C. "Form Perception, Innate Form Preferences and Visually-Mediated Head Turning in Human Newborns." Paper presented at a conference of the Society for Research in Child Development, Denver, 1975.

Graham, P. U., Chir, B., and Rutter, M. "Organic Brain Dysfunction and Child Psychiatric Disorder." *British Medical Journal*, 1968, *3*, 695–700.

Hammond, J. "Hearing and Response in the Newborn." *Developmental Medicine and Child Neurology*, 1970, *12*, 3–5.

Kearsley, R. "Iatrogenic Retardation: A Syndrome of Learned Incompetence." In R. Kearsley and I. Sigel (Eds.), *Infants at Risk: Assessment of Cognitive Functioning.* Hillsdale, N.J.: Erlbaum, 1979.

Kennell, J. H., and others. "Maternal Behavior One Year After Early and Extended Post-Partum Contact." *Developmental Medicine and Child Neurology*, 1974, *16*, 172–179.

Kenner, L. "Autistic Disturbances of Affective Contact." *The Nervous Child*, 1943, *2*, 217–240.

Klaus, M., and Kennell, J. *Maternal–Infant Bonding: The Impact of Early Separation on Loss and Family Development.* St. Louis, Mo.: Mosby, 1976.

Koch, R., and de la Cruz, F. (Eds.). *Down's Syndrome (Mongolism): Research, Prevention and Management.* New York: Brunner/Mazel, 1975.

Mahler, M. "On the First Three Subphases of the Separation–Individuation Process." *International Journal of Psychoanalysis,* 1972, *53,* 333–338.

Mahler, M., Pine, F., and Bergman, A. *The Psychological Birth of the Human Infant.* New York: Basic Books, 1975.

Messer, S. B., and Lewis, M. "Social Class and Sex Differences in the Attachment and Play Behavior of the Year-Old Infant." *Merrill-Palmer Quarterly,* 1972, *18,* 295–306.

Molnar, G. E. "Analysis of Motor Disorder in Retarded Infants and Young Children." *American Journal of Mental Deficiency,* 1978, *83* (3), 213–222.

Mordock, J. "The Separation–Individuation Process and Developmental Disabilities." *Exceptional Children,* 1979, *20,* 176–184.

Mosey, A., Foley, O., McCrae, M., and Thomas, T. *Attachment–Separation–Individuation Observation Scale.* Pennsylvania Department of Education (unpublished paper), 1980.

Murphy, L. B. *Vulnerability, Coping, and Growth from Infancy to Adolescence.* New Haven, Conn.: Yale University Press, 1976.

Osofsky, J., and Connors, K. "Mother–Infant Interactions: An Integrative View of a Complex System." In J. Osofsky (Ed.), *Handbook of Infant Deveopment.* New York: Wiley, 1979.

Parke, R. "Perspectives on Father–Infant Interactions." In J. Osofsky (Ed.), *Handbook of Infant Development.* New York: Wiley, 1979.

Pines, M. "Superkids." *Psychology Today,* January 1979, 53–63.

Prechtel, H. "The Mother–Child Interaction in Babies with Minimal Brain Damage." In B. M. Foss (Ed.), *Determinants of Infant Behavior.* Vol. 2. New York: Wiley, 1963.

Richardson, S. A. "The Socialization of the Blind Child." In A. Goslin (Ed.), *Handbook of Socialization: Theory and Research.* Chicago: Rand McNally, 1969.

Sameroff, A. J. "Early Influences on Development: Fact or Fancy?" In S. Chess and A. Thomas (Eds.), *Annual Progress in Child Psychiatry and Child Development.* New York: Brunner/Mazel, 1976.

Sameroff, A. J., and Chandler, M. "Reproductive Risk and the Continuum of Care-taking Casualty." In F. D. Horowitz, M. Hetherington, and S. G. Siget (Eds.), *Review of Child Development Research.* Chicago: University of Chicago Press, 1975.

Schlesinger, H. "The Hearing Impaired Pre-Schooler." In N. Enger and K. Gain (Eds.), *Social and Emotional Development: The Pre-Schooler.* New York: Walker, 1978.

Schlesinger, H., and Meadow, K. "Development of Maturity in Deaf Children." *Exceptional Children,* 1972, *38,* 461–467.

Segal, J., and Yahraes, H. *A Child's Journey.* New York: McGraw-Hill, 1978.

Simenson, R., Huntington, G., and Barse, S. "Expanding the Developmental Assessment of Young Handicapped Children." In J. Gallagher (Ed.), *New Directions for Exceptional Children: Young Exceptional Children,* no. 3. San Francisco: Jossey-Bass, 1980.

Solnit, A., and Provence, S. "Vulnerability and Risk in Early Childhood." In J. Osofsky (Ed.), *Handbook of Infant Development.* New York: Wiley, 1979.

Solnit, A., and Stark, M. "Mourning and the Birth of a Defective Child." *Psychoanalytic Study of the Child,* 1961, *16,* 523–537.

Spitz, R. A. *The First Year of Life.* New York: International Universities Press, 1965.

Sroufe, L. "Socioemotional Development." In J. Osofsky (Ed.), *Handbook of Infant Development.* New York: Wiley, 1979.

Sroufe, L., and Waters, E. "The Ontogenesis of Smiling and Laughter: A Perspective on the Organization of Development in Infancy." *Psycholgical Review,* 1976, *83,* 173–189.

Stone, N. W., and Chesney, B. "Attachment Behaviors in Handicapped Infants." *Mental Retardation,* 1979, *16,* 8–12.

Thomas, A., and Chess, S. *Temperament and Development.* New York: Brunner/Mazel, 1977.

Thomas, A., Chess, S., and Birch, H. G. *Temperament and Behavior Disorders in Children.* New York: New York University Press, 1968.

Weinraub, M., Brooks, J., and Lewis, M. "The Social Network: A Reconsideration of the Concept of Attachment." *Human Development,* 1977, *20,* 31-47.

Werner, E. E., Bierman, J. M., and French, F. E. *The Children of Kauai.* Honolulu: University Press of Hawaii, 1971.

Werner, E. E., and Smith, R. S. *Vulnerable, but Invincible: A Longitudinal Study of Resilient Children and Youth.* New York: McGraw-Hill, 1981.

Wolff, P. H. "Observations on Newborn Infants." *Psychosomatic Medicine,* 1959, *21,* 110-118.

Wolff, P. H. "Mother-Infant Relations at Birth." In J. G. Howels (Ed.), *Modern Perspectives in International Child Psychiatry.* New York: Brunner/Mazel, 1971.

Yarrow, L. J. "Historical Perspectives and Future Directions in Infant Development." In J. Osofsky (Ed.), *Handbook of Infant Development.* New York: Wiley, 1979.

Yarrow, L. J., Rubenstein, J. L., Pederson, F. A., and Jankowski, J. J. "Dimensions of Early Stimulation and Their Differential Effects on Infant Development." *Merrill-Palmer Quarterly,* 1972, *18,* 205-218.

Zigler, E., and Harter, S. "The Socialization of the Mentally Retarded." In A. Goslin (Ed.), *Handbook of Socialization: Theory and Research.* Chicago: Rand McNally, 1969.

Gordon Ulrey is an assistant professor of clinical psychology at the University of Colorado Health Sciences Center and director of psychology at the John F. Kennedy Child Development Center.

Social interactions with other children play a significant role in development.

The Development and Role of Child–Child Social Interactions

Michael J. Guralnick

Knowledge of the cognitive and language development of young children has provided an important developmental framework for both theoreticians and practitioners. It has also served as a useful guide to the design of intervention strategies for young handicapped children. Too often, however, intervention programs have neglected the social world of the child, particularly the social world of other children. Unquestionably, improvements in cognitive and language development will enhance social development as well; all of these processes are interrelated. The broader concept of communicative development, incorporating language, is clearly linked to social behavior. Yet each process, while subject to varying influences and in turn exerting its own direct and indirect effects on other domains, remains to some degree separable from other processes. A complete understanding of development and the design of intervention strategies must consider the interdependence of cognitive, social, affective, and communicative processes. (See Lewis and Cherry, 1977, for a more complete discussion of models relating to these interrelationships.) However, social development, especially in relation to other children, can and should be identified and studied also as a separate domain.

From the perspective of intervention, a major barrier to efforts to promote child–child social interactions has been a general absence of developmental research in this area. Early work in the 1930s (Bridges, 1933; Maudry and Nekula, 1939; Parten, 1932, 1933) provided detailed descriptions of peer relations of normally developing children in various social situations. This research was followed by an extensive period of inactivity. As a consequence, until quite recently knowledge of the course, characteristics, and organization of peer relations has not been available. Despite the recent burst of activity in this area, the absence of developmental information and a developmental perspective to promote peer relations and social development remains a prominent inadequacy of intervention strategies (Furman, 1980). Even today, information concerning child–child interactions of handicapped children is virtually nonexistent. To add to these difficulties, an extensive array of assessment instruments to measure cognitive and language processes and milestones has been developed; but there is still little interest in, as well as considerable inconsistency among, tests or test items purporting to assess social interactions among children (Guralnick and Weinhouse, forthcoming [a]).

One of the primary reasons for the period of research inactivity in the area of peer relations was a belief in the primacy of parent–child — particularly mother–child — interactions. The centering of the family life–social structure around the mother–child bond contributed to the neglect of other social interactions. In addition, early peer-related work stressed the negative qualities of peer interactions. This negative focus, combined with interpretations of Piaget's (1926) concept of egocentrism suggesting that young children's social interactions are limited, further supported the contention that neglect of peer relations would not significantly impair an understanding of social development.

The publication of Lewis and Rosenblum's (1975a) volume on friendship and peer relations marked the beginning of a rather remarkable resurgence of interest in this area. The interest was fostered by many factors, including a recognition that disordered peer relationships in childhood are associated with later adjustment problems (Cowen and others, 1973) and indications that peer relationships in the preschool years are not as egocentric (Shatz and Gelman, 1973) nor as negative, even during infancy, as first thought (Vincze, 1971). In addition, the social structure of family life changed substantially. More and more children experienced group care at earlier ages and in the process demonstrated that children not only can but do have a social life beyond that with the mother (Belsky and Steinberg, 1978). The advent of early intervention programs for disadvantaged and handicapped children similarly raised new issues involving peer–peer interactions (Tjossem, 1976; Zigler and Trickett, 1978). Finally, the practice of mainstreaming at the early childhood level, with social interactions of handicapped and nonhandicapped children a primary concern, has generated further interest (Guralnick, 1978a. Guralnick, forthcoming [a]).

These changes have resulted in the construction of developmental models that provide broader conceptualizations of social development, models that can readily incorporate peer interactions (Lewis and Feiring, 1979). Theoretical and empirical support has emerged for the notion that interactions with peers actively contribute to social and total development. This increased interest in children's social life has been so dramatic that investigators such as Hartup (1978) have been able to state with confidence that "peer relations occupy a central position in child development. Adequate peer relations contribute to the acquisition of basic social and communicative skills in a manner that interactions with adults cannot or will not produce. The centrality of peer interaction in childhood socialization needs to be better recognized by both research workers and practitioners" (p. 31). The purpose of this chapter is to examine these propositions from the perspectives of both nonhandicapped and handicapped children.

Early Peer Interactions

The search for the roots of child–child social behavior has extended well into the period of infancy. Researchers tracking the developmental course of peer-related social behavior have discovered considerable regularities and consistencies (Mueller and Vandell, 1979). Peer-directed behaviors include social touching at three to four months, smiling and vocalization at six months, and—with the emergence of mobility at six to nine months—the behaviors of approaching, reaching, and following one's playmates. By the age of one year, children appear to have in place all of the fundamental components for complex peer-related social behavior, including imitating; vocalizing and smiling reciprocally; and offering, showing, and giving toys. It should be noted that the term *peer* refers to children of similar chronological ages and with presumably similar skills.

It is extremely difficult to distinguish in very young children between simple exploratory behavior and social behavior in which some social response can be anticipated. Nevertheless, as Mueller and Vandell (1979) suggest, the behavior patterns and apparent reciprocity of infants at six months of age seem to mark the beginning of what is generally considered socially interactive behavior with peers. The characteristics of these infant–infant behaviors, as well as efforts to identify such "true" social behaviors, can be found in a recent study by Vandell and others (1980). These investigators applied Mueller and Brenner's (1977) definition of toddler social behavior. To qualify as an infant–infant social interaction, a behavior must include a discrete act of looking at a peer accompanied by some other form of behavior (touching, smiling). These

behaviors are referred to as socially directed behaviors (SDBs). SDBs by interacting children and that occur within five seconds of each other form a social
unit. Using this framework, researchers can examine the content of SDBs,
including vocalizations, aggressive behaviors (hitting, pushing), touching,
object-related social acts (showing, taking, offering a toy), and approaches.
Moreover, SDBs can be classified as simple (looking plus another social
behavior) or coordinated (looking plus two concurrent social behaviors — for
instance, touching and smiling).

Utilizing these definitions, Vandell and others (1980) observed age-
mate dyads of infants at six, nine, and twelve months of age. Their results
revealed that even for very young children, socially directed behaviors were
quite extensive. Two unit exchanges (Child 1 SDB–Child 2 SDB) were most
common, with children being successful nearly half the time in eliciting social
responses from their companions. Vocalizations occurred at a frequency more
than twice that of any other behavior, and about half the SDBs were classified
as coordinated. Interestingly, the interactions could be best characterized as
prosocial in overall quality, although, as noted, they were typically brief two-
unit exchanges. Most surprising, perhaps, was the finding that relatively few
changes in types of social interactions were observed during the first year of
life. The frequencies of social approach, object-related social acts, and coordinated SDBs did increase, however, as did the percentage of coordinated SDBs.
Peer touching declined significantly. Perhaps it is necessary to look beyond the
first year for significant developmental growth in the number of SDBs, their
length, and their complexity, as well as for the emergence of other important
peer-related social behaviors. The fact that dyads were unfamiliar with each
other may also have masked possible developmental changes.

Toddler Period

Participation of toddler-age children in play groups as well as their
involvement in group care have permitted observations to occur in a wide
range of settings. For example, Holmberg (1980) examined the developmental
changes in social-exchange patterns across six age groups of 1- to 3½-year-olds
enrolled in various daycare centers. Holmberg observed during free-play
activities both positive initiations and elaborated interchanges (the latter defined
as at least two turns for each of two interacting individuals, either child–child
or adult-child), and found an important developmental shift. The number of
positive initiations to other children steadily increased from twelve to forty-
two months. However, after approximately twenty-four months, the frequency of elaborated interchanges to peers increased substantially from a relatively low level and continued to increase in a linear fashion over time thereafter. Consequently, it seems that the skills of young children developed suffi-

ciently in this two-year period for the beginnings of sustained social interactions with peers to occur.

Interestingly, in Holmberg's study the frequency of both positive initiations and elaborated interchanges between children and adults (both child- and adult-initiated) in the setting remained unchanged over this extended period of time. Apparently, adults were adjusting both their frequency of initiations and their responsiveness in such a manner that the total number of interactions was maintained at a relatively constant level. That is, adults initiated most of the interactions at early ages, but as the child's skill in this area increased, a corresponding reduction in the adult initiations occurred. Similarly, adults apparently maintained the level of elaborated interactions by adjusting their response patterns to the capacities of the developing children. Moreover, adults rarely failed to respond to a child's initiations, but the proportion of unsuccessful child–child encounters was more variable. Finally, it should be noted that in contrast to elaborated interchanges, simple interchanges (a two-turn unit of initiate/respond [I/R]) did not vary widely across the thirty-month span for child–child interactions. In fact, the only major changes occurred between twelve and eighteen months. As Vandell and others (1980) noted, these simple I/R patterns were reasonably well established even in infancy.

Additional insight into developmental changes occurring during this period was obtained in a longitudinal study of play group interactions conducted by Mueller and Brenner (1977). These investigators focused on a play group formed for children of seventeen months with no prior peer experience. The group met daily in the morning for six months until the children were twenty-three months old. Their results were similar to Holmberg's (1980): The frequency of I/R units increased during the period from seventeen to nineteen months of age but remained stable thereafter. Apparently, an initial acquaintanceship period is needed to create the proper conditions for I/R interactions to emerge in the play group setting. More dramatic and consistent changes were noted, however, for coordinated SDBs, which increased three-fold over the five-month period. Moreover, longer interactions (similar to Holmberg's elaborated interchanges) increased predictably over time.

Another significant change that appears to occur in the second year is a substantial increase in peer-initiated interactions when both peers and adults are available. In fact, in some circumstances (for instance, in a laboratory setting in which children can interact with a peer, the mother, or toys), interactions with mothers declined while contacts with toys and peers increased (Eckerman and others, 1975). In other circumstances (for instance, free play in a group-care setting), adult-directed interactions remained relatively stable (especially after eighteen months of age), while peer initiations increased considerably (Holmberg, 1980). Although factors such as the behavioral setting, available toys, familiarity of playmates, and related variables can influence the balance between adult-directed and peer-directed interactions, the developmental shift during the toddler period seems well established (Mueller and Vandell, 1979).

Consequently, it appears that prior to the second year, children have already developed the component behaviors necessary for peer social interactions, and they successfully engage in simple I/R exchanges. During the second year, substantial increases in the capability of children to engage in sustained interactions with peers emerges, along with a corresponding increase in the complexity of their socially directed behaviors. These, in turn, permit more elaborate social exchanges to occur, particularly after about two years of age. In addition, a willingness for and interest in participation in social exchanges with peers increases. This attitude ultimately develops into a preference for interaction with peers under nonstressful circumstances.

To determine how such growth comes about, researchers must examine the content and skills that are associated with these developmental changes. Engaging in sustained interactions, in particular, requires children to behave in a more reciprocal fashion, to adjust the form and content of their interactions to those of their companions, and to be sensitive to various contextual factors that regulate social exchanges.

Content and Developing Skills

Some of the earliest work in the field suggests that much of the content of peer interactions during the toddler period is negative (Maudry and Nekula, 1939). Although struggling over toys and other negative behaviors clearly characterize many peer interaction episodes, more recent investigations do not support these early conclusions (Eckerman and others, 1975; Holmberg, 1980; Lewis and others, 1975). Recent research indicates that even infants show a remarkably low level of antagonistic acts toward their peers (Vandell and others, 1980). Prosocial behaviors during the toddler period, especially distal ones such as vocalizing, smiling, and gesturing, are the predominant forms of interaction and constitute the content of most exchanges. Direct involvement in social play often consists of showing, offering, accepting, coordinating, and taking toys. As the child develops, verbalizations account for increasing proportions of the content of child–child interactions (Finkelstein and others, 1978), and the general content of these verbalizations becomes more and more similar to adult–child exchanges (Holmberg, 1980).

The growth of verbal interaction skills that are associated with increased peer-directed social interaction was investigated in a study by Mueller and others (1977). These investigators observed that the percentage of utterances that received a verbal response during play group activities increased from 27 percent to 64 percent between the ages of twenty-two and thirty months. In an

effort to evaluate the factors that contributed to this increased social responsiveness, the researchers assessed a number of predictor variables of the speaker,
including content (relevant or not relevant), speaker attention (on peer, not on
peer), distance (less or more than three feet), attention getting (present or
absent), and listener attention (on speaker, not on speaker). Their analyses
revealed that the increase in social responsiveness noted above from twenty-
two to thirty months of age was correlated with significant changes in each of
these variables. Changes were in the direction of the first behavior in each set
of parentheses, with the exception of attention getting, which changed toward
less of a need to utilize attention-getting techniques. Accordingly, it appears
that more mutual and reciprocal relationships between interactors accompany
increases in social interactions, along with a more appropriate selection of
message content.

A final ability that appears to correspond with developmental changes
during this period consists of a cluster of what are perhaps best referred to as
turn-taking skills. Mueller and Lucas (1975) observe that reciprocal imitation,
"act/watch" sequences, and the development of complementary roles are important elements for promoting interaction in toddler play groups. Through these
turn sequences the child seemingly gains an element of control over frequently
unpredictable social objects and forms the rudiments of a rule structure for
discourse that becomes elaborated as verbal skills become more sophisticated.

Comparisons Between Adult–Child
and Child–Child Interactions

The concept of a social network that includes peer relations as an essential component has given rise to a number of hypotheses regarding the relationship between child–child and adult–child interactions. As outlined by
Vandell (1980), one possibility is that peer-directed behaviors are derivative of
earlier and more fundamental adult-directed social behaviors. For example,
turn-taking sequences and other alternation patterns that may relate to later
conversational skills are well established in early infancy (Bruner, 1974/1975;
Stern, 1977). A second, contrasting hypothesis is that the two "systems" are
distinct, each having different origins and functions. Finally, it is conceivable
that adult–child and child–child interactions are separate manifestations of
similar underlying processes.

These hypotheses provided a framework for an important experimental effort by Vandell (1980) designed to examine the origin of peer interactions. Observing infants interacting at six, nine, and twelve months of age
with their mothers and age-mates in a playroom setting, Vandell employed a
variety of correlational techniques and other comparisons to evaluate which
hypothesis provided the best fit to the data. Not unexpectedly, a simple rela-

tionship was not found. Infant–infant interactions were different from mother–child exchanges in terms of frequency of smiles, vocalizations, and touching. However, there seemed to be a common underlying element of what can be referred to generally as "sociability," reflected by the positive correlation between infants' social behavior (smiling, vocalizing) to both mothers and infant playmates at various times.

Perhaps the most reasonable hypothesis is that an identifiable tendency to respond to social objects (sociability) characterizes children at early ages. The level of sociability varies widely from individual to individual but tends to remain fairly stable both in the short term (Vandell, 1980) as well as over more extended periods of time (Waldrop and Halverson, 1975). Recent research suggests that a particular level of sociability may be attributed to the quality of socioemotionally based parent–child interactions as well as to temperament (Chess, 1979). Reports by Easterbrooks and Lamb (1979), Lieberman (1977), and Waters and others (1979) suggest that peer social competence is directly related to the security of maternal attachment. (See also Suomi, 1979, for a primate analogue to these hypotheses.)

If we continue this line of thought and we assume a particular level of social and emotional development (perhaps best conceptualized as competence), we can posit that peer interactions and exploratory behaviors emerge in infancy and take different forms according to the demands of the companion and the setting. During this time, more proximal behaviors (for instance, touching) are directed toward the mother and more distal ones (for instance, vocalization and looking) are directed toward peers (Vandell, 1980). For toddlers, differential responding is still apparent, with more motor behaviors directed toward peers than toward adults (Mueller, 1979). Parent–child interactions tend to take on a directive, preplanned quality, whereas the establishment and, in part, maintenance of peer relations seem more dependent on fortuitous circumstances, which frequently involve toys. The adult–child and child–child systems may become even more differentiated from each other with experience, that is, with further differentiation of the forms of behavior between companions. It is possible that these interactions with different companions begin to influence each other as well (Vandell and Mueller, 1980). Thus, peer experiences may create developmental patterns not entirely shared by the adult–child system. This finding in turn suggests that each system may serve different developmental functions. What these functions might be will be considered shortly.

Peer Influences

The possibility that experience with one's peers is an essential condition for the growth and development of certain social skills has been investigated in two important studies. Mueller and Brenner (1977), working with toddlers at age twelve months, established a play group consisting of six dyads that met each morning for seven months. To evaluate the effects of the play group experience, the researchers established a comparison play group consisting of seventeen-month-old children who had had limited previous peer experience. Comparisons between these two groups at comparable ages revealed differences along two critical dimensions: coordinated socially directed behaviors and long social interactions (chains of three SDBs or more). Although various forms of social interaction increased over time for both play groups, the effects of peer experience were manifested in greater complexity of social behaviors as well as in skills that enabled the children to sustain a social exchange.

A similar outcome was obtained in a short-term longitudinal study of nine-month-old infants (Becker, 1977). Examining the interactions of infants paired for ten sessions, Becker observed considerable social interaction among peers at the outset, which increased further over the ten sessions. Significant increases in the frequency of I/R units were obtained as well as increases in coordinated SDBs. No changes were observed for a control group of infants that were not provided with additional peer experience. Thus, growth in peer-directed behavior apparently resulted from the peer experience itself and not from maturational or other related factors.

Taken together, these two studies indicate that certain forms of peer interaction develop directly as a result of peer experience. At this time it is possible only to speculate what it is about peers that can produce these changes. Some insight into the process can, however, be obtained from the work of Holmberg (1980), in which clear differences emerged between the organization of child–child and adult–child interactions. As noted in a previous section, in child–adult early interactions it is the adult who initiates and in general controls the interaction. Coequal status was the rule for child–child interactions at all ages, but the ability to coordinate and sustain elaborated social interactions with peers did not develop until after the second year. Apparently, practice in the development of initiation and maintenance skills with partners (that is, peers) who provide greater degrees of unpredictability is essential. Moreover, as Lewis and Rosenblum (1975b) point out, the element of pacing may be highly relevant. They note, "In its developing relationship with peers, the infant has the opportunity for paced, slowly elaborating enlargement of communicative, aggressive, defensive, and cooperative skills" (p. 6). Hartup (1978) also emphasizes that the coequal status of the relationship is critical for the development of peer-related social skills. Consequently, despite the fact that it is not known exactly at this time how such processes operate, these findings clearly suggest certain unique characteristics of the coequal relationship among peers.

Preliminary evidence suggests that beyond promoting the development of social skills and social interactions, active involvement with peers can also enhance the constructiveness of children's play. Rubenstein and Howes (1976) compared toddlers' play at home in the presence of a familiar playmate to those play occasions when only the child's mother was available. The most important effect noted was that the presence of a playmate was associated with a higher level of play with objects. The essentials of this study were replicated in a recent and more extensive investigation comparing children reared at home and children exposed to daycare settings (Rubenstein and Howes, 1979). Children participating in daycare showed significantly greater competence in play than children reared at home. Examination of the contexts within which play occurred in the daycare setting revealed that peer presence was significantly correlated with increased levels of play.

What might account for this effect? Although no definitive answer can be put forth, Rubenstein and Howes (1976) suggest the following: "Our speculation is that previously acquired skills with inanimate objects become elaborated or integrated at more complex levels of behavior in the context of imitating and being imitated by a peer and in the context of being reinforced by the shared pleasure of a shared activity" (p. 602).

Preschool Years

The rather sophisticated social skills that have developed during the toddler years become elaborated and intertwined with the complex social and play group structures that form during the preschool years. Social interactions with peers become more frequent, more diverse, and more complex (Field, forthcoming; Goldman, 1976; Holmberg, 1980). Preferences for certain peers and for interacting with children of the same sex and age also become more marked. Quarrelling and aggressive behaviors tend to occur and may even increase, particularly for boys, during various parts of the preschool period. Nevertheless, the overall level of negative behavior is quite small in comparison to positive interactions. Prosocial behaviors, such as helping, being affectionate, and showing sympathy, tend to increase during this time, although not very rapidly (Goldman, 1976; Yarrow and Waxler, 1976).

The pioneering work of Mildred Parten (1932) at the Nursery School of the Institute of Child Welfare, University of Minnesota, was designed to characterize various aspects of the social participation of preschool children and has become a classic in the field. Parten constructed a set of social participation categories for play referred to in developmental sequence as unoccupied, solitary, onlooker, parallel, associative, and organized supplementary or cooperative. The value of this system resided in its ability to capture the critical differentiating elements of various forms of social participation among children.

Utilizing this system, Parten observed the behavior of 2- to 4½-year-olds in a cross-sectional study. She found that solitary and parallel play were dominant at 2 to 3 years, but even for children 2½ to 3 years old considerable involvement in associative play was noted. The most dramatic developmental change appeared at age 3 as a substantial increase in cooperative play, which remained at a high level. Steady increases in solitary play were somewhat evident across the age span studied, but changes in parallel play were variable, remaining reasonably high at all age levels. Only the very youngest children engaged in noticeable amounts of unoccupied behavior.

The existence of a developmental hierarchy is implicit in Parten's (1932) discussions; in Parten's hierarchy individual children progress through the different forms of social participation. Smith (1978) examined this assumption by noting the transitions of individual children from one predominant form of social participation to another over a nine-month period. Only the younger children in Smith's preschool groups followed the "classical" Parten pattern. Others, usually older, seemed to bypass a dominant stage of parallel interactions and moved from solitary play directly to a form of group play. It is possible that older children, having more experience with age mates, do not need parallel play as a prerequisite to group play (Mueller and Brenner, 1977). This finding calls into question the assignment of solitary play to a developmentally immature state.

In a recent study, Bakeman and Brownlee (1980) also question the progressive character of Parten's stages. These investigators analyzed short-term transitions of three-year-old children from one level of social participation to another. Their analysis revealed that substantial changes did indeed occur from moment to moment and in many different directions. The authors suggest that for children 2½ to 3½ years old, parallel play may be a useful strategy to facilitate their participation in group activities. It is important to note that investigations of these momentary transitions provide a perspective somewhat different from but not necessarily in conflict with studies assessing the predominant forms of children's social participation.

As Roper and Hinde (1978) pointed out, an additional assumption of the Parten scheme is that short-term consistency of behavior (individual correlations of children's social participation at two points in time), as well as cross-situational consistency (that is, individual child correlations between indoor and outdoor play), should be evident. As measured by rank-order correlations (Roper and Hinde, 1978), this consistency does exist. Such cross-situational consistency does not imply that different situations do not affect the qualitative and quantitative aspects of social participation. Social play varies considerably with the setting and materials available (Guralnick, in press [a]; Mueller, 1979; Rogers-Warren and Wedel, 1980; Shure, 1963). Additional research confirms that curriculum model (Reuter and Yunik, 1973), teacher/child ratio (O'Connor, 1975), and classroom structure (Huston-Stein and others, 1977) also affect peer-related social participation. However, despite these momentary changes, overall social participation ordered among children tends to remain relatively stable from one global situation to another.

Despite questions concerning the generality of the developmental sequences, the Parten scale has clearly stood the test of time as a useful description of the categories and development of social participation. It provides a valuable description of shifts in modal qualities of play for both individuals and groups and appears to be a reliable and useful measure for disturbed as well as normal children (Wintre and Webster, 1974).

Ironically, both the researchers who have questioned the accuracy of placing parallel and solitary play on a social-participation continuum and those who have questioned the relative immaturity of solitary play have helped to establish the utility of the Parten scale by stimulating research that suggests the scale's value can be enhanced by joining it with the cognitive dimension of constructiveness of play. Moore and others (1974) found that solitary play for kindergarten children tended to be associated with independence and maturity rather than with immature forms of behavior. A similar outcome was obtained by Rubin and others (1976), who combined the cognitive play scales of Smilansky (1968) with the Parten scale. This work suggests that solitary play is not immature behavior; in fact, parallel play seems a lower level of social-cognitive play. In consequence, it appears that the play of preschool children can be described most adequately by combining constructiveness of play measures with measures of social participation. When these two measures are used, the results reveal that, although solitary play, for example, decreases with age, its constructiveness can take many forms, with the least advanced forms also decreasing with age (see Rubin and others, 1978).

Reciprocity and Mutuality

The skills associated with advancement in social participation, particularly associative and cooperative play, are perhaps best understood in relation to the development of reciprocity and mutuality (Cairns, 1979). The concept of reciprocity has many dimensions, but it generally reflects a tendency to achieve a balanced interaction with one's companion. The most straightforward illustration of this balance is the correspondence between the frequency of a child's giving and receiving social interactions. This correlation is well established during the preschool years and remains high even as the number of social interactions increases (Charlesworth and Hartup, 1967; Greenwood and others, 1977). However, it is not the quantitative aspects alone that reflect a reciprocal relationship; the qualitative ones do also. The concept of reciprocity includes adjustments that elicit similarities in response as related to content, style, and even length of utterances, as well as to complementary forms of interacting, as in question-answer sequences (Cairns, 1979). For example, friendly and positive initiations tend to be met with friendly and positive responses, while demanding initiations are countered by coercive replies (Leiter, 1977). Moreover, reciprocity is strengthened by the tendency of children to seek out companions whose interactions are similar to their own (Kohn, 1966) and by the balance that results between interacting children when choice of playmate is limited (Cairns, 1979).

Mutuality refers to the maintenance of social contact through the use of various strategies. The concepts of mutuality and reciprocity must be considered together when one moves beyond the surface features of initiation/response units and considers the diverse and complex social skills required to sustain long interchanges and to carry out interpersonal goals. The key to maintaining such social sequences consists of mastering an array of social and conversational skills, all of which demand moment-to-moment adjustments in one form or another (Guralnick, forthcoming [b]). Such skills and strategies include: recognizing and using appropriate social conventions, identifying relevant context cues, gauging the knowledge and skills of playmates, utilizing techniques for maintaining the interest of companions, and reestablishing social contact when the interaction wanes. The learning of these skills occurs rapidly during the preschool period, as suggested by Mueller's (1972) research on the forms of meaningful social interchange in the conversations of preschool children, Garvey's (1975, 1977) work on requests for action and contingent queries, as well as the investigations of Spilton and Lee (1977) on conversational adjustments that occur in the face of communicative failure. The development of reciprocity and mutuality during this time is sufficient to keep pace with the increased complexity of play, the advanced forms of social participation children engage in, the variety of social contexts in which social contact occurs, and the diverse number of playmates contacted.

Preference and Similarity

Study of early peer relationships shows that children seek out peers with similar characteristics, skills, and styles of interacting (Lewis and others, 1975; Rubin, 1980; Vandell and Mueller, 1980). As children establish these preferences, the variations and adjustments needed to maintain reciprocity and mutuality become less taxing, since many of the playmates' interactions become more predictable. Encountering children who are significantly different, however, requires the child to work harder to maintain a balance in the interaction. Moreover, the types of strategies and skills needed to maintain mutuality are likely to be different for children with dissimilar abilities or interests, both in terms of their qualitative and quantitative characteristics.

Mixed-Age Interactions

Social exchanges between children of different ages may provide opportunities for social development not found in same-age interactions. The older child may benefit from the experience of accommodating to the varying cognitive and social skills of the younger companion. Research by Allen (1976) suggests that older children benefit from tutoring experiences because they must organize, present, and clarify information in cross-age situations. At the same time, the younger child is stimulated by interaction with older, more skillful children and challenged to develop more advanced forms of social and communicative behavior. Older children, since they share characteristics of both adults and same-age children, may be in a position to create unique learning experiences. They may be more responsive than same-age peers but less dominating in social situations than adults. In addition, although often adopting certain adult roles, older children remain children and are likely to engage their companion in play activities that are not naturally a part of adult–child relationships. Finally, the older child may serve as a secure guide for exploring new environments.

Although speculations regarding the functions and positive benefits of mixed-age interactions are intriguing, even the relatively few studies that have been conducted create a complex and often conflicting pattern of results. For example, comparing the social behavior of children in mixed-age classrooms in contrast to same-age classrooms, Goldman (1976) found that both three- and four-year-olds in the mixed-age classrooms interacted more positively and engaged in more solitary play but spent less time in parallel play and teacher-directed activities compared to three- and four-year-olds in same-age classrooms. Goldman interpreted these results as indicating that more mature forms of social interaction occurred in the mixed-age settings. However, in a laboratory study, Lougee and others (1977) found that social activity was reduced for the older child in a mixed-age dyad, although it was higher for the younger companion. Moreover, considerable variability across pairs of children was evident. To add to the complexity, Langlois and others (1978) found that the social behavior of younger boys in mixed-age dyads of three- to five-year-olds was reduced. Examining the nature of the dyadic interactions more closely, these researchers concluded that because of this substantial age difference the five-year-olds adopted a more adult and dominant role by directing the interaction. As a result, the younger children spent much of their time complying, but engaging in little verbal or related social interaction. Interestingly, however, this pattern was not obtained in dyads of girls (see also Jacklin and Maccoby, 1978).

Even the relationships of infant- and toddler-age children create different same-age and mixed-age patterns. Lewis and others (1975) observed that more imitation, more body contact, and more frequent expressions of positive affect occurred during mixed-age than during same-age interactions. The investigators suggest that these differences may reflect a difference in the functions of these two sets of interactions. Similarly, observations of young children and their older preschool siblings suggest that the older siblings can facilitate mastery of the object environment (Lamb, 1978a, 1978b). The younger children tend to monitor closely the actions of their siblings and imitate them, while older siblings tend to offer objects, take objects and exhibit nurturant forms of behavior.

It appears from this research that mixed-age situations create different behavior patterns than same-age situations, but the developmental significance of these differences remains unclear (Hartup, 1978). In addition, the setting and the magnitude of the age differences may modulate substantially the effects of these mixed-age interactions. A more consistent and favorable developmental picture emerges, however, with a more detailed examination of adjustments in the content of social exchanges in mixed-age settings. In a now classic study, Shatz and Gelman (1973) found that when four-year-olds interacted with two-year-olds, the older children carefully adjusted the complexity and other important features of their speech to the cognitive and linguistic levels of their listeners. Not only did the adjustments facilitate communication, but also the linguistic environment the four-year-olds provided the two-year-olds may have been favorable to the acquisition of language by the younger children. Addition research on conversational responsiveness (Masur, 1978) and functional aspects of speech (Gelman and Shatz, 1977) confirms that mixed-age interactions produce substantial and seemingly appropriate adjustments on the part of the older child. However, whether the linguistic and communicative environment created by these adjustments does in fact influence the development of the younger child is not yet established.

Peer-Related Social Development of Handicapped Children

Do handicapped children follow the same sequence of development in relation to child–child social interactions as normally developing children? At a particular developmental level, is the level of child–child social interactions what would be expected from a normative perspective? How do different handicaps affect social interactions with peers? What is the role of peer experience in the development of peer relations of handicapped children? What types of peer experiences might best facilitate the development of peer relations of handicapped children? Unfortunately, these and many other questions cannot be answered with any degree of certainty, since virtually no research has been carried out in these areas. Such questions have been asked rarely. Historically, interest has focused on the handicapped child's social interactions with parents and teachers, and developmental questions have centered around the child's cognitive growth.

The dramatic increase in early intervention programs, as well as efforts to mainstream young handicapped children, have substantially altered this state of affairs. Issues regarding the peer relations of handicapped children now arise daily in classrooms and group-care centers across the country. For this reason, there is a need for both theoretical and practical research in this area, but there have been only two preliminary studies addressing some of these issues. Both studies focus on the social development of relatively homogeneous groups of children in segregated settings.

In the first study, Field (1980) made preliminary observations of three classrooms of three- and four-year-old handicapped children. Although the children were grouped homogeneously in each of the three classrooms by severity of handicap (severe, moderate, and minimal), the types of handicaps within each group appeared heterogeneous and consisted of perceptual-motor handicaps, general developmental delays, cerebral palsy, and speech and hearing deficits. In addition, a group of nonhandicapped children, similar in chronological age and therefore developmentally more advanced, was observed. To achieve more complete matching across developmental levels, a group of older handicapped children was observed.

The frequency of occurrence of isolated social behaviors, such as looking, smiling, vocalizing, touching, hitting, and offering and sharing toys, was observed for children in each of the classrooms. Unexpectedly, very few differences in these peer-directed behaviors were observed among the handicapped groups. Only the frequency of looking at peers was ordered across the groups (minimal > moderate > severe), although the minimally handicapped children remained in closer proximity to their peers than either the moderately or severely handicapped children. The normally developing three- to four-year-old children, however, exhibited many more socially directed behaviors toward peers in a variety of categories than any of the handicapped groups. When Field compared the social behaviors of the older handicapped children (who were similar in developmental age to the normally developing children) to those of the normally developing children, Field found the handicapped group vocalized less and was less frequently in physical proximity to peers. A similar comparison was made between two handicapped groups matched in terms of developmental level (an older group with severe handicaps and a younger, less delayed group). This comparison revealed that the younger but less severely handicapped group vocalized more and was in greater proximity to peers than the older and more severely handicapped group.

Consequently, as compared to normally developing children, handicapped children lag considerably behind in peer-related social development than what one might expect from their developmental levels. Also, severity of handicap appears to be correlated more strongly with delays in peer-related interactions than with any other factor. The advantages of chronological age and corresponding experience are apparently overridden by severity of handicap.

Perhaps the limited differences in peer-related behavior among the three handicapped groups are in part explained by the relatively isolated and nonsequential social behavior categories used in this study. Future researchers might benefit from using more complex social interaction measures and longitudinal and cross-sectional analyses. A clearer perspective of the processes of social development might be obtained by tracing over time the developmental changes in an individual.

A related approach to this problem was taken in a study by Guralnick and Weinhouse (forthcoming [b]). In an initial effort to trace more comprehensively and more closely the developmental patterns of handicapped children, over 100 developmentally delayed children enrolled in typical community preschool programs were observed. In these community programs children were divided by chronological age and severity of handicap into two broad groupings. There were fifteen classes of the lower functioning and generally younger group, referred to as Early Training (ET), and twelve classes of more advanced children, referred to as Preschool (PS). The groups were observed at the beginning and the end of the school year while the children were engaged in free play. The average chronological age for the ET group was approximately thirty-nine months; the mean age for the PS group was fifty-four months. Developmental assessments revealed that the ET children were predominantly severely and moderately delayed. In addition, a substantial number of these children manifested associated and significant motor and sensory deficits. The PS children, however, were primarily moderately or mildly delayed and had no accompanying significant motor or sensory handicaps.

Although the detailed results of this study are complex and extensive, they do indicate that peer-related social behaviors develop in a sequence that tends to parallel that of normally developing children. Rates of change differed substantially between ET and PS children for virtually all measures and within certain subgroups, but clear growth was observed even for ET children. Comparisons of these data with data from studies of younger normally developing children, as well as comparisons with corresponding developmental measures, also suggest that handicapped children lag behind nonhandicapped in peer-related interactions even when developmental levels are similar.

Mainstreaming

The development of peer-related social behaviors is constrained, in large part, by the skills of playmates. Those assessing the development of such behaviors must keep these constraints in mind. Unresponsive and unskilled companions can only have the effect of limiting or depressing the levels of social interaction. Because the data gathered by Field (1980) and Guralnick and Weinhouse (forthcoming [b]) were derived from interactions taking place in segregated and relatively homogeneous settings, the outcomes and developmental patterns are limited to an unknown extent by that circumstance. Recent efforts to mainstream handicapped preschool children constitute one approach to counteract potential deleterious effects of social separation (Guralnick, 1978a). Although the concept and practice of mainstreaming extend beyond the process of facilitating social development (Guralnick, forthcoming [c]); Sarason and Doris, 1979), social interaction constitutes its most fundamental component.

When considering the processes of social integration and development for certain groups of handicapped children, the researcher encounters a perplexing problem. Placement in well-designed mainstreamed settings should provide children better models for social development, more responsive playmates, greater opportunities to experience adaptive consequences, and more frequent opportunities to encounter diverse social situations (Guralnick, 1978b). Unfortunately, the degree of social integration, that is, the extent of social interaction occurring between handicapped and nonhandicapped children, is not very substantial for children with more severe handicaps (Guralnick, in press [d]). The social exchanges of the majority of the more severely handicapped children tend to be limited to a smaller number of children with similar handicaps.

It is possible, however, that even relatively limited social exchanges among children at different developmental levels or with varying severity of handicaps could be beneficial. Most of the available research indicates that very few negative interactions occur in mainstreamed settings. This finding suggests that opportunities for observational learning may be greater than those derived from direct social exchanges (Guralnick, 1980, in press [d]). Moreover, the situation is quite positive for mildly handicapped children, since most studies indicate that social integration (and presumably any benefits derived from those social exchanges) is virtually complete (Dunlop and others, 1980; Guralnick, 1980; Ispa and Matz, 1978).

Recent research examining the influence of a child's playmates on social behavior, although limited and somewhat fragmentary, has nonetheless identified a number of critical concerns and issues. For example, in a recent study, Guralnick (in press [e]) compared social participation, constructiveness of play, social/communicative interactions, and certain teacher behaviors as functions of the heterogeneity of the play group. The sample studied consisted of three groups of handicapped preschool children with primary and developmental delays (mildly, moderately, and severely handicapped) and one group of nonhandicapped children. At the beginning and the end of the school year, Guralnick compared children's interactions in homogeneous play groups to their interactions in heterogeneous play groups. The homogeneous groups consisted of a group of nonhandicapped and mildly handicapped children and a group of moderately and severely handicapped youngsters. The heterogeneous groups were composed of children from all four developmental levels. The results indicated that the levels of social participation and constructiveness of play, as well as the frequency of social/communicative behaviors, increased over the school year. The only effect caused by varying the composition of the play group was a reduction in the inappropriate play of the severely handicapped children.

Although it is perhaps reassuring to some that social interaction with peers was not disrupted by integration of the groups, it may be distressing to others that only a limited positive impact was observed. Related research (Novak and others, 1980) suggests that the social behaviors of handicapped youngsters are more similar to those of normally developing children when the handicapped children are enrolled in mainstreamed as opposed to segregated settings. In the study by Novak and others, however, as well as in virtually all others designed to compare the effects of segregated versus mainstreamed experiences, investigators have been forced for practical reasons to study intact groups. Consequently, assignment of children to groups, teacher–child ratio, curriculum, and so on, usually are not controlled. This lack of control is a confounding factor and permits numerous alternative explanations for the results obtained.

Vandell and George (in press) carried out a laboratory study from a somewhat different perspective. They compared mixed dyads of hearing-impaired and normal-hearing children with similar dyads of just hearing-impaired and just normal-hearing children. Interestingly, the number of social interactions did not differ among the groups. However, the amount of time spent engaging in social interaction, the mean duration of interaction, and the percentage of successful initiations were greater in both kinds of unmixed dyads than in the mixed dyads. Nevertheless, differences in social interactions between the hearing-impaired dyads and the mixed dyads were relatively small on an absolute basis (24.7 percent versus 16.6 percent for percentage of time of session involving social interaction; 11.8 seconds versus 9.3 seconds for the mean duration of an interaction; and 56.2 percent versus 42.3 percent for successful initiations). These results suggest that more similarities than differences exist.

Examination of the qualitative aspects of interactions when they occur is a more indirect approach to determining whether the characteristics of playmates can affect social interactions. To ensure effective communication, nonhandicapped children must make considerable social and communicative adjustments when interacting with children of different ages and developmental levels. If these adjustments are successful, they may facilitate the development of social/communicative competence. Research reviewed in the section on mixed-age interactions suggests that normally developing children may provide such an appropriately adapted and progressive environment for younger children. Should nonhandicapped children also be able to adjust their social/communicative interactions to children similar in chronological age but at a different developmental level, important indirect evidence for the potential value of the heterogeneous grouping of children would be obtained.

This possibility was investigated in a series of studies by Guralnick and Paul-Brown (1977, 1980, forthcoming). These analyses of the speech of nonhandicapped children as addressed to mildly, moderately, and severely handicapped companions revealed the existence of a number of important adjustments, which reflected awareness of the various developmental levels of the handicapped companions. When addressing children with severe handicaps, nonhandicapped children simplified their speech by using fewer complex utterances and reducing the mean length of utterance. Moreover, their speech was less diverse, less frequent, contained more repetitions, and included a variety of functional and discourse devices to maintain contact and probe for understanding. An important finding was that speech was not uniformly simplified to a lower level but contained sufficient diversity in both content and complexity to facilitate communication and at the same time provide a challenging linguistic and communicative environment.

Additional evidence for the effectiveness of social/communicative encounters was obtained from an examination of techniques nonhandicapped children employed to gain compliance from handicapped companions after an unsuccessful attempt to do so. In general, the advanced children creatively and persistently pursued clarification of an initial behavior request by using a wide range of specific adaptive behaviors (justifying, adding relevant information, simplifying request, prompting companion). The adjustment of nonhandicapped children to children at different developmental levels includes modification in syntax, semantics, functional uses, and discourse characteristics of their speech. These adjustments support the hypothesis that communication is effective and interactions between handicapped and nonhandicapped children can facilitate the social/communicative development of the handicapped companion.

To reach these conclusions, Guralnick and Paul-Brown interpreted the appropriateness of the adjustments by nonhandicapped children in light of knowledge about adjustments made by parents of normally developing children. These adjustments by parents facilitate the communicative development of normally developing children (Broen, 1972; Gleason and Weintraub, 1978; Snow, 1972). The adjustments made by nonhandicapped to handicapped children are remarkably similar to these parental modifications, which, in turn, are consistent with the adjustments preschool children make to even younger children (Shatz and Gelman, 1973). However, the positive effects of mixed-level peer interaction applies only to children with general developmental delays. For children with other handicaps, such as sensory or orthopedic disabilities, an entirely different framework must be used to assess the appropriateness of any adjustments. Certain adjustments with respect to gestures and complexity of instructions might be required, for example, to achieve effective communication with hearing-impaired children. Unfortunately, the available research indicates that these adjustments by nonhandicapped children do not occur (Arnold and Tremblay, 1979; Vandell and George, in press).

It appears, then, that in play groups that are developmentally heterogeneous, appropriate adjustments occur among children. These adjustments may facilitate communicative development and, thereby, social interaction. It is important to keep in mind, however, that the available research shows the qualitative characteristics of social/communicative interactions of nonhandicapped children in heterogeneous groups to be more nearly like adult–child interactions than child–child exchanges. It particular, the social exchanges of nonhandicapped children and children with more severe delays were often dominated by more advanced children; they made the majority of the adjustments, were primarily responsible for sustaining the interactions, and utilized discourse features and other conversational devices commonly employed by adults. Clearly, coequal status did not characterize these interactions.

While a rich linguistic and social environment provided by nonhandicapped classmates may have many important benefits for handicapped children, arrangements must be made to ensure that interactions with coequals also occur. To develop skills in initiating and maintaining social interactions, children require the give-and-take that is part of coequal social exchanges. The possibility does exist, however, that matching children of similar developmental levels (an older handicapped child and a younger normally developing child) may create ideal conditions for promoting this form of social development. In such a match, interactions would be more coequal, and handicapped children might benefit additionally from the higher levels of responsivity and diversity that are likely to be displayed by the nonhandicapped children. Although there is some evidence that this strategy can be extremely successful for withdrawn children (Furman and others, 1979), the value of mainstreamed programs in promoting social development and social interactions remains largely unknown (Guralnick, in press [a], in press [d]).

Implications for the Handicapped Child: Future Directions

Developmental models provide important guides for most early intervention programs. No such model, however, has been widely applied to the domain of child–child interactions. The newly emerging developmental information regarding peer relations should form an essential framework for understanding and promoting the peer relations of handicapped children. To be effective, however, this knowledge must be supplemented with information obtained from direct observations of handicapped children in a variety of settings. Research regarding the peer relations of young handicapped children can identify unique barriers to peer-related social development and suggest the types of instructional strategies that might be most useful. Similarly, the typical course of development may be modified significantly by the social responsiveness and interpersonal characteristics of playmates. Unfortunately, despite the dramatic increases in both conceptual and empirical knowledge about the child–child social interactions of normally developing children, only limited information of a corresponding nature exists about handicapped children.

Curriculum design should be informed by knowledge about peer-related developmental patterns and general developmental milestones and by questions that probe how such social interactions are organized, what strategies children employ most effectively in social exchanges, and what factors affect the rate and quality of these interactions. Appropriate and corresponding assessment instruments are necessary companions to curriculum design. It has been noted earlier, however, that such instruments are presently inadequate and often contradictory. When these instruments are considered as possible frameworks for designing instructional programs, their inadequacies are further underscored. Accordingly, a major task for the future is to organize into a useful curriculum the developmental information obtained from handicapped as well as nonhandicapped populations and to design associated assessment instruments.

The complexity of this effort cannot be overstated. Not only are social behaviors extremely sensitive to situational variables, but also the interpersonal behavior style and personality characteristics of children are likely to color social behavior assessments even more markedly than they do other assessments, such as cognitive assessments. (See Zigler, 1973, for discussions of motivational factors and their relation to performance variables, including cognitive testing.) Questions regarding what social skills exist, what elements in the social repertoire might be missing, what factors might be inhibiting the use of already existing skills, or what behaviors might be creating social isolation will test the limits of a practitioner's diagnostic-assessment skills. Certainly the overlaps among the domains of behavior disorders, clinical child psychology, and social development are apparent.

Perhaps the most perplexing issue for those assessing handicapped children and implementing comprehensive programs in the area of peer-related social development is the problem of social motivation. Many handicapped children, particularly those with severe deficits, tend to have little interest in social exchange. How children come to view social objects as rewarding in and of themselves or as means to goods and services is a fundamental and unanswered question in developmental psychology. That social interactions form the basis for developing social competence and gaining information and knowledge about the world is a fact that needs no elaboration. Nevertheless, contingency — that is, building successful experiences to enable the child to master and predict both the object and social environment — seems essential. To bring such contingency about, caretakers must properly interpret the child's interactive attempts, be highly responsive, and carefully tune their adjustments. Because similar social experiences with peers are no less important, especially in light of the fact that such relationships display many characteristics unique to peer–peer social interactions, the significance of providing an interactive and responsive peer environment is evident.

Discussion of peer-related social development inevitably includes issues related to other developmental domains as well as to other areas of clinical and educational interest. This fact reflects the interrelatedness of all the child's developing skills and abilities. Nevertheless, the importance of interactions with other children should not be underestimated. Systematic attention to child–child social interactions is needed for the design of strategies to promote development. Without such systematic attention to the peer environment, we can have no truly comprehensive understanding of the handicapped child.

References

Allen, V. L. (Ed.). *Children as Teachers: Theories and Research on Tutoring.* New York: Academic Press, 1976.

Arnold, W., and Tremblay, A. "Integration of Deaf and Hearing Preschool Children." *Journal of Communication Disorders,* 1979, *12,* 245–251.

Bakeman, R., and Brownlee, J. R. "The Strategic Use of Parallel Play: A Sequential Analysis." *Child Development,* 1980, *51,* 873–878.

Becker, J. M. T. "A Learning Analysis of the Development of Peer-Oriented Behavior in Nine-Month-Old Infants." *Developmental Psychology,* 1977, *13,* 481–491.

Belsky, J., and Steinberg, L. D. "The Effects of Day Care: A Critical Review." *Child Development,* 1978, *49,* 929–949.

Bridges, K. M. B. "A Study of Social Development in Early Infancy." *Child Development,* 1933, *4,* 36–49.

Broen, P. A. "The Verbal Environment of the Language-Learning Child." *American Speech and Hearing Association Monograph,* 1972, *17* (entire issue).

Bruner, J. S. "From Communication to Language: A Psychological Perspective." *Cognition,* 1974/75, *3,* 255–287.

Cairns, R. B. *Social Development: The Origins and Plasticity of Interchanges.* San Francisco: W. H. Freeman, 1979.

Charlesworth, R., and Hartup, W. W. "Positive Social Reinforcement in the Nursery School Peer Group." *Child Development,* 1967, *38,* 993–1002.

Chess, S. "Developmental Theory Revisited: Findings of Longitudinal Study." *Canadian Journal of Psychiatry,* 1979, *24,* 101–112.

Cowen, E. L., Pederson, A., Bibigian, H., Izzo, L. D., and Trost, M. A. "Long-Term Follow-Up of Early Detected Vulnerable Children." *Journal of Consulting and Clinical Psychology*, 1973, *41*, 438–446.

Dunlop, K. H., Stoneman, Z., and Cantrell, M. L. "Social Interaction of Exceptional and Other Children in a Mainstreamed Preschool Classroom." *Exceptional Children*, 1980, *47*, 132–141.

Easterbrooks, M. A., and Lamb, M.E. "The Relationship Between Quality of Infant–Mother Attachment and Infant Competence in Initial Encounters with Peers." *Child Development*, 1979, *50*, 380–387.

Eckerman, C. O., Whatley, J. L., and Kutz, S. L. "Growth of Social Play with Peers During the Second Year of Life." *Developmental Psychology*, 1975, *11*, 42–49.

Field, T. M. "Self, Teacher, Toy, and Peer-Directed Behaviors of Handicapped Pre-School Children." In T. M. Field, S. Goldberg, D. Stern, and A. M. Soster (Eds.), *High-Risk Infants and Children: Adult and Peer Interactions*. New York: Academic Press, 1980.

Field, T. M. "Early Peer Relations." In P. Strain (Ed.), *The Utilization of Classroom Peers as Behavior Change Agents*. New York: Plenum, forthcoming.

Finkelstein, N. W., Dent, C., Gallagher, K., and Ramey, C. F. "Social Behavior of Infants and Toddlers in a Day-Care Environment." *Developmental Psychology*, 1978, *14*, 257–262.

Furman, W. "Promoting Social Development: Developmental Implications for Treatment." In B. B. Lahey and A. E. Kazdin (Eds.), *Advances in Clinical Child Psychology*. New York: Plenum, 1980.

Furman, W., Rahe, D. R., and Hartup, W. W. "Rehabilitation of Socially Withdrawn Preschool Children Through Mixed-Age and Same-Age Socialization." *Child Development*, 1979, *50*, 915–922.

Garvey, C. "Requests and Responses in Children's Speech." *Journal of Child Language*, 1975, *2*, 41–63.

Garvey, C. "The Contingent Query: A Dependent Act in Conversation." In M. Lewis and L. A. Rosenblum (Eds.), *Interaction, Conversation, and the Development of Language*. New York: Wiley, 1977.

Gelman, R., and Shatz, M. "Appropriate Speech Adjustments: The Operation of Conversational Constraints on Talk to Two-Year-Olds." In M. Lewis and L. A. Rosenblum (Eds.), *Interaction, Conversation, and the Development of Language*. New York: Wiley, 1977.

Gleason, J. B., and Weintraub, S. "Input Language and the Acquisition of Communicative Competence." In K. Nelson (Ed.), *Children's Languages*. Vol. 1. New York: Gardner, 1978.

Goldman, J. A. "The Social Participation of Preschool Children in Same-Age vs. Mixed-Age Groupings." Unpublished doctoral dissertation, University of Wisconsin, 1976.

Greenwood, C. R., Walker, H. M., Todd, N. M., and Hops, H. *Normative and Descriptive Analysis of Preschool Free Play Social Interactions*. CORBEH Report No. 29. Eugene: Center at Oregon for Research in the Behavioral Education of the Handicapped, University of Oregon, 1977.

Guralnick, M. J. (Ed.). *Early Intervention and the Integration of Handicapped and Nonhandicapped Children*. Baltimore: University Park Press, 1978a.

Guralnick, M. J. "Integrated Preschools as Educational and Therapeutic Environments: Concepts, Design, and Analysis." In M. J. Guralnick (Ed.), *Early Intervention and the Integration of Handicapped and Nonhandicapped Children*. Baltimore: University Park Press, 1978b.

Guralnick, M. J. "Social Interactions Among Preschool Children." *Exceptional Children*, 1980, *46*, 248–253.

Guralnick, M. J. "Programmatic Factors Affecting Child–Child Social Interactions in Mainstreamed Preschool Programs."*Exceptional Education Quarterly*, in press (a).

Guralnick, M. J. "Peer Influences on the Development of Communication Competence." In P. Strain (Ed.), *The Utilization of Classroom Peers as Behavior Change Agents.* New York: Plenum, forthcoming (b).

Guralnick, M. J. "Mainstreaming Young Handicapped Children." In B. Spodek (Ed.), *Handbook of Research on Early Childhood Education.* New York: Free Press, forthcoming (c).

Guralnick, M. J. "The Efficacy of Integrating Handicapped Children in Early Education Settings: Research Implications." *Topics in Early Childhood Education*, in press (d).

Guralnick, M. J. "The Social Behavior of Preschool Children at Different Developmental Levels: Effects of Group Composition." *Journal of Experimental Child Psychology*, in press (e).

Guralnick, M. J., and Paul-Brown, D. "The Nature of Verbal Interactions Among Handicapped and Nonhandicapped Preschool Children." *Child Development*, 1977, *48*, 254–260.

Guralnick, M. J., and Paul-Brown, D. "Functional and Discourse Analyses of Nonhandicapped Preschool Children's Speech to Handicapped Children." *American Journal of Mental Deficiency*, 1980, *84*, 444–454.

Guralnick, M. J., and Paul-Brown, D. *Sequential Analyses of Communicative Episodes Among Children at Different Developmental Levels*, forthcoming.

Guralnick, M. J., and Weinhouse, E. M. *Child–Child Social Interactions: An Analysis of Assessment Instruments*, forthcoming (a).

Guralnick, M. J., and Weinhouse, E. M. *Peer Related Social Interactions Among Handicapped Children: Their Development and Characteristics*, forthcoming (b).

Hartup, W. W. "Peer Interaction and the Process of Socialization." In M. J. Guralnick (Ed.), *Early Intervention and the Integration of Handicapped and Nonhandicapped Children.* Baltimore: University Park Press, 1978.

Holmberg, M. C. "The Development of Social Interchange Patterns from 12 to 42 Months." *Child Development*, 1980, *51*, 448–456.

Huston-Stein, A., Friedrich-Cofer, L., and Susman, E. J. "The Relation of Classroom Structure to Social Behavior, Imaginative Play, and Self-Regulation of Economically Disadvantaged Children." *Child Development*, 1977, *48*, 908–916.

Ispa, J., and Matz, R. D. "Integrating Handicapped Preschool Children Within a Cognitively Oriented Program." In M. J. Guralnick (Ed.), *Early Intervention and the Integration of Handicapped and Nonhandicapped Children.* Baltimore: University Park Press, 1978.

Jacklin, C. N., and Maccoby, E. E. "Social Behavior at Thirty-Three Months in Same-Sex and Mixed-Sex Dyads." *Child Development*, 1978, *49*, 557–569.

Kohn, M. "The Child as Determinant of His Peers' Approach to Him." *The Journal of Genetic Psychology*, 1966, *109*, 91–100.

Lamb, M. E. "Interactions Between Eighteen-Month-Olds and Their Preschool-Aged Siblings." *Child Development*, 1978a, *49*, 51–59.

Lamb, M. E. "The Development of Sibling Relationships in Infancy: A Short-Term Longitudinal Study." *Child Development*, 1978b, *49*, 1189–1196.

Langlois, H. J., Gottfried, N. W., Barnes, B. M., and Hendricks, D. E. "The Effect of Peer Age on the Social Behavior of Preschool Children." *The Journal of Genetic Psychology*, 1978, *132*, 11–19.

Leiter, M. P. "A Study of Reciprocity in Preschool Play Groups." *Child Development*, 1977, *48*, 1288–1295.

Lewis, M., and Cherry, L. "Social Behavior and Language Acquisition." In M. E. Lewis and L. A. Rosenblum (Eds.), *Interaction, Conversation, and the Development of Language.* New York: Wiley, 1977.

Lewis, M., and Feiring, C. "The Child's Social Network: Social Object, Social Functions, and Their Relationship." In M. Lewis and L. A. Rosenblum (Eds.), *The Child and Its Family.* New York: Plenum, 1979.

Lewis, M., and Rosenblum, L. A. (Eds.). *Friendship and Peer Relations.* New York: Wiley, 1975a.

Lewis, M., and Rosenblum, L. A. "Introduction." In M. Lewis and L. A. Rosenblum (Eds.), *Friendship and Peer Relations.* New York: Wiley, 1975b.

Lewis, M., Young, G., Brooks, J., and Michaelson, L. "The Beginning of Friendship." In M. Lewis and L. A. Rosenblum (Eds.), *Friendship and Peer Relations.* New York: Wiley, 1975.

Lieberman, A. F. "Preschoolers' Competence with a Peer: Relations with Attachment and Peer Experience." *Child Development,* 1977, *48,* 1277-1287.

Lougee, M. D., Grueneich, R., and Hartup, W. W. "Social Interaction in Same- and Mixed-Age Dyads of Preschool Children." *Child Development,* 1977, *48,* 1353-1361.

Maudry, M., and Nekula, M. "Social Relations Between Children of the Same Age During the First Two Years of Life." *The Journal of Genetic Psychology,* 1939, *54,* 193-215.

Masur, E. F. "Preschool Boys' Speech Modifications: The Effect of Listeners' Linguistic Levels and Conversational Responsiveness." *Child Development,* 1978, *49,* 924-927.

Moore, N. V., Evertson, C. M., and Brophy, J. E. "Solitary Play: Some Functional Reconsiderations." *Developmental Psychology,* 1974, *10,* 830-834.

Mueller, E. "The Maintenance of Verbal Exchanges Between Young Children." *Child Development,* 1972, *43,* 930-938.

Mueller, E. "(Toddlers + Toys) = (An Autonomous Social System)." In M. Lewis and L. A. Rosenblum (Eds.), *The Child and Its Family.* New York: Plenum, 1979.

Mueller, E., Bleir, M., Krakow, J., Hejedus, K., and Cournoyer, P. "The Development of Peer Verbal Interaction Among Two-Year-Old Boys." *Child Development,* 1977, *48,* 284-287.

Mueller, E., and Brenner, J. "The Growth of Social Interaction in a Toddler Playgroup: The Role of Peer Experience." *Child Development,* 1977, *48,* 854-861.

Mueller, E., and Lucas, T. "A Developmental Analysis of Peer Interaction Among Toddlers." In M. Lewis and L. A. Rosenblum (Eds.), *Friendship and Peer Relations.* New York: Wiley, 1975.

Mueller, E. C., and Vandell, D. "Infant-Infant Interaction." In J. Osofsky (Ed.), *Handbook of Infant Development.* New York: Wiley, 1979.

Novak, M. A., Olley, J. G., and Kearney, D. S. "Social Skills of Children with Special Needs in Integrated and Separate Preschools." In T. M. Field, S. Goldberg, D. Stein, and A. M. Sostek (Eds.), *High-Risk Infants and Children: Adult and Peer Interactions.* New York: Academic Press, 1980.

O'Connor, R. D. "The Nursery School Environment." *Developmental Psychology,* 1975, *11,* 556-561.

Parten, M. B. "Social Participation Among Preschool Children." *Journal of Abnormal Social Psychology,* 1932, *27,* 243-269.

Parten, M. B. "Social Play Among Preschool Children." *Journal of Abnormal Social Psychology,* 1933, *28,* 136-147.

Piaget, J. *The Language and Thought of the Child.* New York: Harcourt Brace Jovanovich, 1926.

Reuter, J., and Yunik, G. "Social Interaction in Nursery Schools." *Developmental Psychology,* 1973, *9,* 319-325.

Rogers-Warren, A., and Wedel, J. W. "The Ecology of Preschool Classrooms for the Handicapped." In J. J. Gallagher (Ed.), *New Directions for Exceptional Children: Ecology of Exceptional Children,* no. 1. San Francisco: Jossey-Bass 1980.

Roper, R., and Hinde, R. A. "Social Behavior in a Play Group: Consistency and Complexity." *Child Development,* 1978, *49,* 570-579.

Rubenstein, J., and Howes, C. "The Effects of Toddler Interaction with Mother and Toys." *Child Development,* 1976, *47,* 597–605.

Rubenstein, J. L., and Howes, C. "Caregiving and Infant Behavior in Day-Care and in Homes." *Developmental Psychology,* 1979, *15,* 1–21.

Rubin, K. H., Maioni, T. L., and Hornung, M. "Free Play Behaviors in Middle- and Lower-Class Preschoolers: Parten and Piaget Revisited." *Child Development,* 1976, *47,* 414–419.

Rubin, K. H., Watson, K. S., and Jambor, T. W. "Free Play Behaviors in Preschool and Kindergarten Children." *Child Development,* 1978, *49,* 534–536.

Rubin, Z. *Children's Friendships.* Cambridge, Mass.: Harvard University Press, 1980.

Sarason, S. B., and Doris, J. *Educational Handicap, Public Policy, and Social History: A Broadened Perspective on Mental Retardation.* New York: Free Press, 1979.

Shatz, M., and Gelman, R. "The Development of Communication Skills: Modifications in the Speech of Young Children as a Function of Listener." *Monographs of the Society for Research in Child Development,* 1973, *38* (5).

Shure, M. B. "Psychological Ecology of a Nursery School." *Child Development,* 1963, *34,* 979–992.

Smilansky, S. *The Effects of Sociodramatic Play on Disadvantaged Preschool Children.* New York: Wiley, 1968.

Smith, P. K. "A Longitudinal Study of Social Participation in Preschool Children: Solitary and Parallel Play Reexamined." *Developmental Psychology,* 1978, *14,* 517–523.

Snow, C. E. "Mothers' Speech to Children Learning Language." *Child Development,* 1972, *43,* 549–565.

Spilton, D., and Lee, L. C. "Some Determinants of Effective Communication in Four-Year-Olds." *Child Development,* 1977, *48,* 968–977.

Stern, D. *The First Relationship.* Cambridge, Mass.: Harvard University Press, 1977.

Suomi, S. J. "Differential Development of Various Social Relationships by Rhesus Monkey Infants." In M. Lewis and L. A. Rosenblum (Eds.), *The Child and Its Family.* New York: Plenum, 1979.

Tjossem, T. D. (Ed.). *Intervention Strategies for High Risk Infants and Young Children.* Baltimore: University Park Press, 1976.

Vandell, D. L. "Sociability with Peer and Mother During the First Year." *Developmental Psychology,* 1980, *16,* 355–361.

Vandell, D. L., and George, L. B. "Social Interaction in Hearing and Deaf Preschoolers: Successes and Failures in Initiations." *Child Development,* in press.

Vandell, D. L., and Mueller, E. C. "Peer Play and Friendships During the First Two Years." In H. C. Foot, A. J. Chapman, and J. R. Smith (Eds.), *Friendship and Social Relations in Children.* New York: Wiley, 1980.

Vandell, D. L., Wilson, K. S., and Buchanan, N. R. "Peer Interaction in the First Year of Life: An Examination of Its Structure, Content, and Sensitivity to Toys." *Child Development,* 1980, *51,* 481–488.

Vincze, M. "The Social Contacts of Infants and Young Children Reared Together." *Early Child Development and Care,* 1971, *1,* 99–109.

Waldrop, M. F., and Halverson, C. F., Jr. "Intensive and Extensive Peer Behavior: Longitudinal and Cross-Sectional Analyses." *Child Development,* 1975, *46,* 19–26.

Waters, E., Wippman, J., and Sroufe, L. A. "Attachment, Positive Affect, and Competence in the Peer Group: Two Studies in Construct Validation." *Child Development,* 1979, *50,* 821–829.

Wintre, M. G., and Webster, C. S. "A Brief Report on Using a Traditional Social Behavior Scale with Disturbed Children." *Journal of Applied Behavior Analysis,* 1974, *7,* 345–348.

Yarrow, M. R., and Waxler, C. A. "Dimensions and Correlates of Prosocial Behavior in Young Children." *Child Development,* 1976, *47,* 118–125.

Zigler, E. "The Retarded Child as a Whole Person." In D. K. Routh (Ed.), *The Experimental Psychology of Mental Retardation*. Hawthorne, N.Y.: Aldine, 1973.

Zigler, E., and Trickett, P. K. "IQ, Social Competence, and Evaluation of Early Childhood Intervention Programs." *American Psychologist,* 1978, *33,* 789–798.

Michael J. Guralnick is director of the Nisonger Center and professor of psychology and communication at Ohio State University.

Teachers must address social competence directly if their mentally retarded
students are to achieve societal integration.

Preparing Mentally Retarded Adolescents for Societal Adaptation

Jon P. Ziarnik

As we have seen in the previous chapters, adaptive social development is an important, complex, and challenging process for anyone. In the mentally retarded child, however, development of appropriate social/emotional behaviors is particularly susceptible to disruption. Several factors work to thwart the social development of such a child: the lowered cognitive ability of a retarded child, social isolation, and environmental support based on stereotypic bias for nonadaptive, inappropriate behaviors. The point of view expressed in this chapter is that social reintegration of the mentally retarded can begin only with the development of those socially acceptable behaviors needed for success in our world today.

The range of services to the mentally retarded found in any society is a direct outgrowth of that society's state-of-the-art treatment technology, as well as cultural norms and value systems (Pollard and others, 1979). The last two decades have seen startling changes in the range, scope, and purpose of services for the mentally retarded. Great strides have been made in the development of appropriate instructional techniques for severely retarded individuals (Bellamy, 1976; Gold, 1972; Karan and others, 1976; Thompson and Grabowski, 1972). These and other studies demonstrate that systematic and data-oriented instructional techniques based on the principles of learning can enable retarded individuals to acquire skills heretofore thought impossible. These demonstrations of skill acquisition in retarded individuals, coupled with a variety of legal decisions (Burgdorf, 1979), have changed our traditional values regarding the disabled. In the past, the service delivery system was designed to isolate or segregate individuals perceived as different. However, the concept of normalization (Nirje, 1969), which is now a philosophical cornerstone of services to the developmentally disabled, has led to increased integration of retarded persons in community-based programs. Education for the mentally retarded also has changed. Instructional techniques and values have evolved, and today education is viewed as an integral part of the continuum of services to the developmentally disabled.

Public Law 94–142, Education for All Handicapped Children Act, reflects the belief that handicapped children must whenever possible be integrated from an early age into regular classrooms. It also reflects the attitude that handicapped children are individuals and that their unique problems and needs must be addressed on an individual basis. The purpose of this chapter is to facilitate the continuum of services to retarded adolescents by providing curriculum guidelines to teachers. Using the guidelines, teachers can help prepare the student for entry into prevocational or vocational training, or the world of work.

Values, Labels, and Treatment Choices

Those providing services to mentally retarded individuals should realize that evaluation methods and treatment strategies are closely linked. The manner in which one perceives an individual and reacts to that individual are nearly inseparable (Merton, 1968). Throughout history there has been a close association between basic concepts of mental retardation and the nature of treatment available to the mentally retarded (Rosen and others, 1977).

White and Wolfensberger (1969) describe the Western concept of mental retardation as closely linked to the moral philosophies of Luther and Calvin, both of whom perceived the mentally retarded as inhabited by Satan. After a long period, characterized largely by indifference, society passed through a stage of "desire" to make deviant individuals not deviant, a period of "concern" during which deviants were sheltered from society, and finally a time of "alarm" during which society was sheltered from the deviant. This time of "alarm," which in the first part of the twentieth century shaped the isolationist concepts of treatment for the mentally retarded, is of central importance for any teacher who wishes to provide adequate programs to the mentally retarded. Individuals are segregated largely on the basis of a societal judgment about the individual's ability to "fit in" (Goffman, 1963). Nearly thirty years ago, Tredgold (1952) suggested that social competence should be the only criterion used to identify the mentally retarded.

Society's judgments of the retarded not only affect federal, state, and local policy (Pollard and others, 1979) but also affect decisions made at the service delivery level as well. When a mentally retarded student enters a classroom, the teacher receives a variety of useful and not so useful information, including educational history and psychometric scores. Because it is used to establish eligibility for the class, this information will likely be the rationale for some sort of student label. Studies suggest that, once labeled (for example, educable mentally retarded), a student is likely to elicit different types of teacher interactions than students labeled normal, trainable, or learning disabled (Palmer, 1979). Palmer (1979) reports that teachers ignored currently equal academic achievement and assigned more remedial curricula to students labeled mentally retarded than to students labeled normal. Although Palmer (1980) presents follow-up data that suggest the label is only one source of information determining teacher judgments and that these judgments (and thus prescriptions) may change with repeated grade-level performance, this finding is challenged by Rosenthal and Jacobson (1968), who report that teachers tended to dislike students who achieved more than their labels predicted.

It appears that those providing services to the mentally retarded have used labels, whether categorical or psychometric, as determinants of services provided and predictors of student performance. In the past it was generally assumed (Olshansky, 1969) that disabled persons could not function in anything but a segregated environment after they left school. Thus, attempts to teach the skills necessary for community integration were viewed as unneccessary (Brown and others, 1978). One central premise of this chapter is that a student label, whether psychometric, categorical or functional, formal or informal, bears no predictive relationship to learning potential (Bellamy, O'Connor, and Karan, 1979). Unless grouping and labeling contribute to a change in the functional level of the student, they have little instructional relevance (Brown, 1973). However, pursuing appropriate instructional goals with a mentally retarded child is a formidable task. Repeated failure has produced interesting coping mechanisms on the part of instructors.

Severence and Gasstrom (1977) found that teachers believed "ability" had more influence on task failure for students labeled mentally retarded than for those labeled normal, whereas they believed "effort" contributed more to task success for students labeled mentally retarded. In other words, students labeled mentally retarded were less likely to be credited for success and were less likely to receive the benefit of the doubt for failure than a nonlabeled student. In this case, the labels caused teachers to evaluate students' similar behaviors differently.

Reevaluating the Locus of the Problem

If the effects of a label are to be reduced, a shift must occur in the focus of evaluation efforts. We must stop viewing the locus of the problem as within the student (that is, the student is severely retarded) and begin to view the problem as one of restructuring the learning experiences to take advantage of student strengths and to minimize student weaknesses. With this shift, environmental conditions become the locus of the problem. There is a practical reason for the shift in the locus of control: There is little a teacher can do about genetic abnormalities, birth defects, or biochemical malfunction.

However, we have considerable evidence that important determinants of skill acqusition are antecedents (what comes before), task structure (what is required), and consequences (what comes after). Moreover, antecedents, task structure, and consequences are all open to direct manipulation by the instructor. With the locus of the problem open to manipulation, the difficulty no longer need be viewed as the student's failure to learn. The new challenge is the instructor's: how to structure learning experiences. This premise suggests that if the student is not learning, changing, or succeeding in a program, the instructor must take responsibility for initiating experiences in which the student can make progress (Ziarnik, 1980).

Establishing Instructional Objectives

Today, the mentally retarded are increasingly integrated into community-based programs where they receive a broad range of services from intense programming to periodic follow-along services. The emerging consensus is that mentally retarded persons can and should live and work in normative settings. As part of the continuum of community-based services, the public school must adapt to this changing emphasis by similarly altering curricula, instructional methods, and goals. In response to Public Law 94–142, virtually every state provides services to low-functioning, mentally retarded children in public schools. However, the adequacy of certain circumscribed instructional objectives emphasizing academic skills must be called into question. Given the recent advances in instructional technology and the great needs of the mentally retarded student, it is extremely difficult to justify academic curricula that at the end of thirteen years produce a student prepared for home maintenance or placement in a traditional residential facility. Schools need to begin to view their role with a mentally retarded student as part of a larger continuum of services, which has changed markedly in the last ten years.

As previously suggested, we have let perceptions, judgments, and outcome expectancies control curriculum choices for the mentally retarded. In general, the curriculum offered is a reflection of our bias toward a logical outcome from school: People will integrate via the world of work. Although work appears to be alternately viewed as unavoidable drudgery or as the cornerstone of self-esteem (Terkel, 1974), it is the vehicle by which most people integrate into the community. However, because of the belief that mentally retarded persons could not function in a postschool work environment other than, at best, a sheltered workshop, few attempts were made to provide them with the skills necessary for community-vocational integration. In light of recent advances in habilitation training, this belief can no longer be considered true. Many authors have demonstrated that the severely mentally retarded can master a variety of vocational skills, such as assembling a nineteen-piece cam switch actuator (Bellamy and others, 1975) or constructing a Tektronix cable harness in seventy-nine steps (Hunter and Bellamy, 1976). Further, the retarded have mastered these skills at a level competitive industry requires of its ordinary workers.

Example One. Bellamy and others (1975) presented data on two clients who were trained to assemble the cam switch actuator. The first client was a male of twenty-six with Down's syndrome who had been institutionalized for fifteen years. He obtained a Vineland Social Quotient of 23 and a Peabody Picture Vocabulary IQ of 10. The second client was a female of twenty-two, institutionalized for eighteen years prior to training. Her Vineland Social Quotient was 19.

Both clients were taught to assemble a nineteen-piece cam switch actuator, which is utilized in electronics assembly. Component parts ranged in size from 3/8 inch in length and 3/16 inch in diameter to 2 ¾ inches in length and 1 inch in diameter. The assembly task involved fifty-one separate steps, which were taught in a forward chain. That is, with each new step, the preceding steps were performed before the trial was reinforced. Success was defined as two sequential perfect trials (fifty-one steps). The first client achieved success in eighty-nine trials, after 8 hours and 38 minutes of training. The second client achieved success in 6 hours and 19 minutes of training.

Similar methodology has been utilized successfully to teach mentally retarded individuals a wide variety of tasks, including independent living skills (*Detailed Progress Report,* 1970; Johnson and Bailey, 1977), assertive skills (Gentile and Jenkins, 1980), and postural training (Sherrill, 1980). The *Detailed Progress Report* (1970) from Parsons State Hospital in Kansas reports consistent success in teaching a wide variety of residential skills, including personal grooming, vocabulary building, communicating, using leisure time, and housekeeping.

Much of this research is being disseminated and integrated into many postschool, community-based programs and in some areas into public schools as well. Although these demonstrations of productive vocational potential are encouraging and important, they indicate a major problem: the general assumption that only skill development is the domain of vocational training programs or schools and that appropriate social and emotional behaviors, which also affect community integration, will be learned elsewhere. While researchers who have produced these exceptional examples of vocational competence would undoubtedly also support the development of social skills, they would likely argue that they are demonstrating success in a circumscribed area and do not claim to offer definitive solutions to the life problems of handicapped clients. However, a major problem develops when these research examples are disseminated and widely "bought" as demonstrations of total competence.

Gold (1975) hypothesizes a competence-deviance theory. The theory suggests that the more vocationally competent a mentally retarded individual becomes, the more deviance society will either overlook or allow. This viewpoint seems to disregard the literature on success in community integration. Mentally retarded individuals come to the attention of society not because of an inability to assemble cam switch actuators, assemble bicycle brakes, perform janitorial tasks, or tell time. Rather, the mentally retarded are singled out for the way they look and act. That is, social/emotional inappropriateness — not skill level on a particular task — is the reason that most mentally retarded come to the attention of society and fail in community integration efforts. It is important that, if the developmentally disabled are to survive in the public sector, they acquire social skills over and above a specific job competence (Rusch, 1979).

Analysis of the reasons for success or failure of a mentally retarded person in full competitive integration overwhelmingly points to social/emotional factors as pivotal determinants (Crawford and others, 1979; McCarver and Craig, 1974). Becker and others (1979) surveyed staff of community-based vocational training programs and found social/emotional factors listed as the dominant reasons for failure to place mentally retarded individuals in jobs. Interestingly enough, though social/emotional factors are identified as important survival skills in public employment, they are not emphasized in prevocational training programs. Mithaug and Hagmeier (in press) surveyed sheltered workshops and found that ability to communicate basic needs and move safely about the shop were essential for entry into sheltered programs, while social skills were rated thirty-seventh in importance. What we know is not often incorporated into our training programs.

From an analysis of the vocational behaviors lacking in clients (Walker, 1969), Krantz (1971) developed a list of behaviors critical for the vocational success of any person. The list includes job getting, job keeping, social living, personal living, and social living competence. Of the nineteen main categories of behavior, seventeen are decidedly social/emotional in nature, while only two have to do with skill level: *produces enough work* and *produces to appropriate quality of standards.*

As pointed out, retarded individuals can be taught to produce at acceptable levels. Several sources (Goldstein, 1964; Halpern, 1973) estimate that the majority of retarded persons have the potential for satisfactory vocational and social adjustment, although this level is rarely attained (McFall, 1966; Tobias, 1970). What begins to emerge is that it is not so much what the retarded person does as how she or he goes about doing it that is important.

Process Versus Product Curriculum Goals

The distinction between a product (what) and a process (how) is perhaps initially confusing. The following case example illustrates the distinction.

Example Two. A teacher is working on time-telling skills with a class of mentally retarded students. The teacher uses a picture of a clock and asks, "Who can come to the board and point to twelve o'clock?" One student loudly proclaims that he can. When given permission by the teacher, he scrapes his chair across the floor, mutters, "I can, I can" several times on his way to the board, taps a student as he passes, and walks bent over with a slow shuffle. He approaches the clock picture and correctly points to twelve o'clock. The teacher responds, "Good job, now you may sit down."

From a strictly skill or product perspective, this was indeed a good job. The student pointed to the correct time. However, the process, or how the student went about pointing to the time, is the real problem for this student. No matter how well time-telling skills are developed, there is little or no hope of integration and acceptance into the community as long as the student's behavior or process remains objectionable or deviant. Thus, a primary longitudinal objective is to teach mentally retarded students socially acceptable behaviors necessary for effective functioning in the community (Bernstein and others, in press; Brown, 1973).

Example Three. Karen was twenty-two and mildly retarded when she came to the attention of the author, then a consultant to a residential facility. Karen had been terminated by the local vocational rehabilitation counselor after she was fired from a second job for her second "behavior incident" in twelve months. From a skill-level perspective, Karen's vocational training placement as a dishwasher had been a success. Except for her "incidents," Karen was considered a good worker. The problem was that periodically Karen would "blow up" and "for no reason" become self-abusive.

Close analysis and interviews of significant others indicated her incidents were closely associated with criticism. A reasonable hypothesis was that a supervisor's criticism of her job performance increased tension, which increased errors, which increased criticism. To escape the criticism, Karen would blow up and subsequently lose her job. By losing her job, Karen ended the criticism and the tension.

Through role playing, residential staff taught Karen to respond in an appropriate verbal manner to criticism by superiors. Additionally, the staff used reinforcement to increase behaviors that corrected any job-related errors that were the basis for the criticism. Training began with role playing, was later extended to the residential unit's kitchen, and finally was conducted in a number of restaurants in the community. This process ensured that her behavior would not be specific to one or two places but would generalize to many environments. Karen was able to control her behavior, received further vocational rehabilitation training, and was subsequently successfully employed as a dishwasher.

Functional Behavior

As used here, the term *functional behaviors* means those behaviors that are (a) needed for an individual to function effectively in potential future environments, (b) increase independent functioning, and (c) are likely to be reinforced by the environment. What a student is taught should be determined by the demands of the present and future natural environments.

Successful habilitation programs support behavior goals that address functional behaviors. This process is very difficult. Many programs' personnel invest considerable time and effort developing exhaustive lists of survival skills to teach to clients. The development of these skills is undeniably important, but it must be remembered that they are of secondary importance to the process, or how the skill is displayed. Additionally, there is no realistic way to generate an exhaustive list of all the functional behaviors a mentally retarded person might need. We may be able to agree on general categories, but specifics are difficult. There are just too many situational and contextual variables to consider.

By attempting to teach everything to everyone, we often dilute well-meaning efforts by keeping students in perpetual training and losing sight of the fact that the student must enter the world. Even if we generate a definitive list of functional behaviors for one community, that list might be of little use in another community. Those behaviors functional in New York City are not necessarily needed or appropriate on a North Dakota farm.

A way around the problem is to view skills as defined in terms of their critical function (Brown and others, 1976; White and Haring, 1976). There are advantages in this approach to functional behaviors beyond directly relating instructional objectives to *where* the student is going and *what* they need when they get there. By defining the critical function or purpose of a skill, we can begin to identify methods of achieving that end without restricting ourselves to traditional behavior patterns.

For example, it would be redundant and uneconomical to attempt to teach a mentally retarded student all the possible names by which a community calls men's and women's restrooms, even though knowing all of the possible names would mean increased integration within the community. It is possible, however, to teach the most common two or three names and then teach clients to ask someone to help when confronted with a new or novel stimulus. Thus, the critical function, appropriate use of restrooms, is achieved; but the form, complete discriminative ability, is altered.

Brown and others (1978) believe that most curricula for mentally retarded students are fallaciously based upon inappropriate theories or models of human development. (See Baer, 1973, for an excellent discussion of the inappropriateness of applying the developmental model to mentally retarded persons.) They suggest the following guidelines for developing functional curricula.

1. Delineate Curriculum Domains. The initial stage of a functional behaviors curriculum would be to delineate the major topics of interest. For the nonhandicapped student, curriculum content is generally divided into major academic subject areas. However, consistent with the orientation that the education of the mentally retarded should reflect the requirements of relatively independent adult functioning, four curricular domains are proposed: domestic living, vocational pursuits, leisure or recreational activities, and community functioning.

2. Delineate Natural Environments. The rationale for this phase of a development strategy is to identify where the particular behaviors along the four domains are likely to occur. Since specific vocational or recreational skills could be performed in any one of many environments, the task here is simply to list those possible environments and the requirements for each.

3. Delineate the Subenvironments. For each broad class of environment (for instance, home), there exist several subenvironments (basement, bathroom, living room). The purpose of this phase is to specify where behaviors are likely to occur.

4. Delineate Activities in the Subenvironment. In every subenvironment in which a severely handicapped student currently functions or might be expected to function, a number of activities might occur. For example, some activities appropriate to a kitchen are cleaning, cooking, and washing hands. The purpose of this phase is to identify the activities that are appropriate for each subenvironment.

5. Assess the Student's Present Behavior. The question here becomes: Can a particular mentally retarded student perform those activities necessary for success in the subenvironment? Efforts should be made here to describe precisely, in a task-analysis fashion, the steps needed to perform each delineated activity.

6. Design and Implement Instructional Programs. Once an activity has been identified, a mentally retarded student must be taught to perform those tasks.. The purpose of this phase of curriculum development is to design and implement the instructional programs necessary to teach severely handicapped students to perform as many of the skills delineated as possible.

Instructional Methodology

The first five steps should lead to the development of curriculum goals that are both realistic and useful for students. However, step six, the design and implementation of a program, involves another series of steps. Once content is delineated, special attention must be given to instructional methodology.

As suggested, it is the process behaviors, or how students go about achieving objectives, that are the initial targets for intervention. It is not initially important for a student to tell time or order a hamburger at a drive-in; what is important is that a student learn to accomplish these tasks in as socially appropriate a fashion as possible. The unique maladaptive process behaviors of a mentally retarded student are not innate. Rather, they are behaviors learned in interaction with environmental antecedents and largely social consequences (Rosen and others, 1977). It is often the instructor's reactions to a student's behavior(s) that help maintain the inappropriate behavior (Bouliew, 1971; Spradlin and Girardeau, 1966). Thus, instructors can unwittingly reinforce maladaptive behavior.

Example Four. Inattention to task is a behavior commonly observed in classes for the mentally retarded. In many cases, the instructor has a hand in shaping and maintaining students' inattention. The following interaction will illustrate:

Darrell is working at his desk. However, he keeps his eyes on his work for at most a minute. Then, he stops, looks up, and smiles until he catches the eye of the instructor as he or she circulates among the eight students in the room. Sometimes it takes the instructor a few seconds, but other times it takes minutes before he or she responds to Darrell's look by saying, "Good job, keep working, Darrell."

In this example, the instructor has placed Darrell on a variable interval schedule of reinforcement for stopping work and looking around. By not understanding the effects of instructor attention on the student's behavior, the instructor inadvertently strengthened a maladaptive response. In order to change the behavior, the instructor needs to pay attention to Darrell when he *is* attending to task.

In the initial stages of intervention, the instruction primarily occurs as the result of ongoing interaction between teacher and student, much as in the above example. In that case, attention to task is a response that needs to be strengthened whenever it occurs. Thus, it is reinforced regularly regardless of the task. Instruction via ongoing interaction occurs because the *how* (for instance, interpersonal approach, vocal volume, posture, or attention to task) can occur at any time. As a result, instruction does not necessarily occur at a scheduled time. Ziarnik (1980) suggests adopting a proactive orientation. Proactive instruction involves "catching" students doing things right as opposed to reacting only when things are going wrong. This means that instructors must specify which behaviors are appropriate and then appropriately reinforce students when those behaviors occur.

Proactive instructional programs contain at least three major components: instructional objectives, curriculum materials, and instructional methodology. The initial portion of this chapter suggests that the priority instructional objectives for mentally retarded adolescents are based on remediation of those socially unacceptable behaviors that make social integration difficult for the student. However, appropriate instructional methodology is critical to the success of habilitation programs. Even the best objectives fail when students are not taught the responses necessary to achieve the objective. Unfortunately, the variety of learning problems exhibited by the mentally retarded student have frustrated many instructors to the point where they give up and distribute materials for arts and crafts. Bellamy, Horner, and Inman (1979); Bernstein and others (in press); Brown (1973); Gold (1972); and Wehman (1976) suggest the following guidelines for instructional methodology to achieve instructional objectives.

1. Address the Task Directly. Too often goals seem to be addressed in a piecemeal or backdoor fashion. For example, if a client has difficulty writing, instruction should relate directly to writing. Copying letters, learning to hold a pencil correctly, and following directions are all related to writing. However, often such a problem is diagnosed as a result of "perceptual-motor difficulties." The instructor then proceeds to train clients to perform tasks—including balancing, copying a variety of figures, and fitting pegs into boards—whose relation to writing is not obvious. The rationale is that such skills are related to writing. There is no reason to assume, however, that the mentally retarded student—or any student, for that matter—will improve in writing by learning to copy circles or rapidly put pegs in and out of a pegboard. The more directly the problem is addressed, the more likely that the mentally retarded student will learn the task. Once a goal or a deficit or a need is identified, break down the task into small units of behavior related to the task. This procedure is known as task analysis.

2. Use Task Analysis. Breaking a social skill or a vocational task into smaller, logically sequenced increments makes the job easier for the student to learn and increases the teacher's probability of success. Small steps of the chain are then gradually linked together to develop a whole skill.

3. Use Structure and Be Consistent. The initial goal in any program is first to gain control of the behavior, second to generalize that behavior to other environments, and third to maintain the behavior in that environment. During the initial stage of instruction, training procedures must be kept consistent if the client is to exhibit maximum performance. This is true for any skill, but is particularly true for process behaviors. Process behaviors are known as operant behaviors. Operants are behaviors that are controlled by their consequences. If consistency is not maximized, the student will be placed on a variable schedule of consequences for appropriate (or inappropriate) behaviors. The net effect is to make new learning more difficult while old, inappropriate behaviors are actually strengthened.

4. **Use a Data-Base Approach to Programming.** Because gains by low-functioning, mentally retarded clients are in small increments, both program evaluation and instructors' perception of success or failure are likely to be quite subjective. Carefully kept records of preinstructional level, instructional progress, and postinstructional level give an objective measure of accountability.

5. **Generalize Behavior.** Methods to generalize the behavior from the instructional site to the natural environment must be planned. It is usually necessary to teach generalization because behavior is situation-specific (Marholin and others, 1976). What we know about the principles of learning tells us that discrimination is more likely to occur than generalization (Holman, 1977). That is, we are most likely to learn it is acceptable to behave in a certain way in only a few locations than we are to learn it is acceptable to behave that way in many different locations. This discrimination occurs particularly in individuals labeled as mentally retarded. One of the clinical descriptions of individuals so labeled is that they are unable to use previously learned skills in new situations (Langone and Westling, 1979). Effective methods of enhancing generalization are to (a) vary where the training occurs, (b) vary who delivers the training, (c) use consequences that are likely to occur in the natural environment, (d) train for skills that are needed, and (e) create a variable system of reinforcement.

Summary

Social competence is clearly an important consideration in the design of any curriculum that seeks to integrate the mentally retarded into the greater society. It has been repeatedly demonstrated that integration will not occur for the retarded person unless socially objectionable behaviors are eliminated and social abilities are developed. The development of curriculum materials that stress social competence must be preceded by attitudinal changes on the part of teachers and other agents of change. Stigmatizing biases have too long determined our intervention goals and strategies. By carefully analyzing the demands of those future environments the mentally retarded student may enter, educators can serve a vital role in the continuum of care.

References

Baer, D. M. "The Control of the Developmental Process: Why Wait?" In J. R. Nesselroade and H. W. Reese (Eds.), *Life-Span Developmental Psychology: Methodological Issues.* New York: Academic Press, 1973.

Becker, K., Widener, Q., and Soforenko, A. Z. "Career Education for Trainable Mentally Retarded Youth." *Education and Training of the Mentally Retarded,* 1979, *14,* 101–105.

Bellamy, T. (Ed.). *Habilitation of Severely and Profoundly Retarded Adults: Reports from the Specialized Training Program.* Eugene: Center on Human Development, University of Oregon, 1976.

Bellamy, T., Horner, R., and Inman, D. P. *Vocational Habilitation of Severely Retarded Adults.* Baltimore: University Park Press, 1979.

Bellamy, T., O'Connor, G., and Karan, O. *Vocational Rehabilitation of Severely Handicapped Persons.* Baltimore: University Park Press, 1979.

Bellamy, T., Peterson, L., and Close, D. "Habilitation of the Severely and Profoundly Handicapped: Illustrations of Competence." *Education and Training of the Mentally Retarded,* 1975, *10,* 74–186.

Bernstein, G., Ziarnik, J. P., Rudrud, E. H., and Czajkowski, L. *Behavioral Habilitation Through Proactive Programming.* Baltimore: Paul H. Brookes, in press.

Bouliew, D. "Do Institutions Maintain Retarded Behavior?" *Mental Retardation,* 1971, *9,* 36–38.

Brown, L. "Instructional Programs for Trainable-Level Retarded Students." In L. Mann and D. Sabatino (Eds.), *The First Review of Research in Special Education.* Vol. 2. Philadelphia: JSE Press, 1973.

Brown, L., Branston, M., Hamre-Nietupski, S., Pumpian, I., Certo, N., and Gruenewald, L. "A Strategy for Developing Chronological Age Appropriate and Functional Curricular Content for Severely Handicapped Adolescents and Young Adults." Unpublished manuscript, Madison Metropolitan School District, Madison, Wisconsin, 1978.

Brown, L., Nietupski, J., and Hamre-Nietupski, S. *The Criteria of Ultimate Functioning and Public School Services for Severely Handicapped Students.* Madison: University of Wisconsin and Madison Public Schools, 1976.

Burgdorf, R. L. *The Legal Rights of Handicapped Persons.* Baltimore: Paul H. Brookes, 1979.

Crawford, J. L., Aiello, J. R., and Thompson, D. E. "Deinstitutionalization and Community Placement: Clinical and Environmental Factors." *Mental Retardation,* 1979, *17* (2), 59–63.

Detailed Progress Report: A Demonstration Program for Intensive Training of Institutionalized Mentally Retarded Girls (Five Year Summary). Parsons: Bureau of Child Research, Parsons State Hospital and Training Center, University of Kansas, June 1965–July 1970.

Gentile, C., and Jenkins, J. O. "Assertive Training with Mildly Mentally Retarded Persons." *Mental Retardation,* 1980, *18* (6), 315–317.

Goffman, E. *Stigma: Notes on the Management of Spoiled Identity.* Englewood Cliffs, N.J.: Prentice-Hall, 1963.

Gold, M. "Stimulus Factors in Skill Training of the Retarded for a Complex Assembly Task: Acquisition, Transfer, and Retention." *American Journal of Mental Deficiency,* 1972, *76,* 517–526.

Gold, M. W. *Try Another Way*. Indianapolis: Film Productions of Indianapolis, 1975. (Film.)

Goldstein, H. "Social and Occupational Adjustment." In H. A. Stevens and R. Heber (Eds.), *Mental Retardation: A Review of Research*. Chicago: University of Chicago Press, 1964.

Halpern, A. "General Unemployment and Vocational Opportunities for EMR Individuals." *American Journal of Mental Deficiency*, 1973, *78*, 123-127.

Holman, J. "The Moral Risk and High Cost of Ecological Concern in Applied Behavior Analysis." In A. Rogers-Warren and S. F. Warren (Eds.), *Ecological Perspectives in Behavior Analysis*. Baltimore: University Park Press, 1977.

Hunter, J. D., and Bellamy, T. "Cable Harness Construction for Severely Retarded Adults: A Demonstration of Training Technique." In T. Bellamy (Ed.), *Habilitation of Severely and Profoundly Retarded Adults*. Eugene: Center on Human Development, University of Oregon, 1976.

Johnson, M. S., and Bailey, J. S. "The Modification of Leisure Behavior in a Half-Way House for Retarded Women." *Journal of Applied Behavioral Analysis*, 1977, *10*, 273-282.

Karan, O., Wehman, P., Renzaglia, A., and Schutz, R. (Eds.). *Habilitation Practices with the Severely Developmentally Disabled*. Vol. 1. Madison: University of Wisconsin, 1976.

Krantz, G. "Critical Vocational Behaviors." *Journal of Rehabilitation*, July–August 1971, *37*, 14-16.

Langone, J., and Westling, D. L. "Generalization of Prevocational and Vocational Skills: Some Practical Tactics." *Education and Training of the Mentally Retarded*, 1979, *14*, 216-221.

McCarver, R. B., and Craig, E. M. "Placement of the Retarded in the Community: Prognosis and Outcome." In N. R. Ellis (Ed.), *International Review of Research in Mental Retardation*. Vol. 7. New York: Academic Press, 1974.

McFall, T. M. "Post-School Adjustment: A Survey of 50 Former Students of Classes for the Educable Mentally Retarded." *Exceptional Children*, 1966, *32*, 633-634.

Marholin, D. II, Siegel, L. J., and Phillips, D. "Treatment and Transfer: A Search for Empirical Procedures." In M. Hersen, R. M. Eisler, and P. M. Miller (Eds.), *Progress in Behavior Modification*. Vol. 3. New York: Academic Press, 1976.

Merton, R. K. "The Self-Fulfilling Prophecy." In R. K. Merton (Ed.), *Social Theory and Social Structure*. New York: Free Press, 1968.

Mithaug, D. E., and Hagmeier, L. D. "The Development of Procedures to Assess Prevocational Competencies of Severely Handicapped Young Adults." *American Association for the Education of the Severely and Profoundly Handicapped Review*, in press.

Nirje, B. "The Normalization Principle and Its Human Management Implications." In R. B. Kugel and W. Wolfensberger (Eds.), *Changing Patterns of Residential Care for the Mentally Retarded*. Washington, D.C.: President's Committee on Mental Retardation, 1969.

Olshansky, S. G. "Examination of Some Assumptions in the Vocational Rehabilitation of the Mentally Retarded." *Mental Retardation*, 1969, *7*, 51-53.

Palmer, D. J. "Regular Classroom Teacher's Attributions and Instructional Prescriptions for Handicapped and Non-handicapped Students." *Journal of Special Education*, 1979, *13*, 325-337.

Palmer, D. J. "The Effect of Educable Mental Retardation Descriptive Information on Regular Teacher's Attributions and Instructional Perceptions." *Mental Retardation*, 1980, *18*, 171-175.

Pollard, A., Hall, H., and Karan, C. "Community Service Planning." In P. Magrab and J. Elder (Eds.), *Planning for Services to Handicapped Persons*. Baltimore: Paul H. Brookes, 1979.

Rosen, M., Clark, G. R., and Kivitz, M. S. *Habilitation of the Handicapped*. Baltimore: University Park Press, 1977.

Rosenthal, R., and Jacobson, L. *Pygmalion in the Classroom.* New York: Holt, Rinehart and Winston, 1968.

Rusch, F. R. "Toward the Validation of Social/Vocational Survival Skills." *Mental Retardation,* 1979, *17* (3), 143–145.

Severence, L. J., and Gasstrom, L. L. "Effects of the Label 'Mentally Retarded' on Causal Explanations for Success and Failure Outcomes." *American Journal of Mental Deficiency,* 1977, *81,* 547–555.

Sherrill, C. "Posture Training as a Means of Normalization." *Mental Retardation,* 1980, *18* (3), 135–138.

Spradlin, J. E., and Girardeau, F. L. "The Behavior of Moderately and Severely Retarded Persons." In N. R. Ellis (Ed.), *International Review of Research in Mental Retardation.* Vol. 1. New York: Academic Press, 1966.

Terkel, S. *Working.* New York: Pantheon Books, 1974.

Thompson, T., and Grabowski, J. *Behavior Modification of the Mentally Retarded.* New York: Oxford University Press, 1972.

Tobias, T. "Vocational Adjustment of Young Retarded Adults." *Mental Retardation,* 1970, *8* (3), 13–16.

Tredgold, A. F. *A Textbook on Mental Deficiency.* Baltimore: Williams and Wilkins, 1952.

Walker, R. "Pounce." In J. Krumboltz and C. Thoresen (Eds.), *Behavioral Counseling: Cases and Techniques.* New York: Holt, Rinehart and Winston, 1969.

Wehman, P. "Vocational Training of the Severely Retarded: Expectations and Potential." In O. Karan, P. Wehman, A. Renzaglia, and R. Schutz (Eds.). *Habilitation Practices with the Severely Developmentally Disabled.* Vol. 1. Madison: University of Wisconsin, 1976.

White, O. R., and Haring, N. G. *Exceptional Teaching: A Multimedia Training Package.* Columbus, Ohio: Merrill, 1976.

White, W. D., and Wolfensberger, W. "The Evolution of Dehumanization in Our Institutions." *Mental Retardation,* 1969, *7,* 5–9.

Ziarnik, J. P. "Developing Proactive Direct Care Staff." *Mental Retardation,* 1980, *18* (6), 289–292.

Jon P. Ziarnik is associate director of community education,
John F. Kennedy Child Development Center, and assistant professor,
Department of Preventive Medicine, at the University of Colorado.

Index